A Very Conscious Universe from Quaternion SuperStandard Theories

Stephen Blaha Ph. D.
Blaha Research

Pingree-Hill Publishing
MMXX

Copyright © 2020 by Stephen Blaha. All Rights Reserved.

This document is protected under copyright laws and international copyright conventions. No part of this book may be reproduced, stored in a retrieval system, or transmitted by any means in any form, electronic, mechanical, photocopying, recording, or as a rewritten passage(s), or otherwise, without the express prior written permission of Blaha Research. For additional information send an email to the author at sblaha777@yahoo.com or call 603-289-5435.

ISBN: 978-1-7345834-3-4

This document is provided "as is" without a warranty of any kind, either implied or expressed, including, but not limited to, implied warranties of fitness for a particular purpose, merchantability, or non-infringement. This document may contain typographic errors, technical inaccuracies, and may not describe recent developments. This book is printed on acid free paper.

Cover: The back cover has a picture of a computer simulation of filaments in the universe. Picture courtesy of Andrew Pontzen and Fabio Governato.

Rev. 00/00/01   June 10, 2020

To Margaret

Some Other Books by Stephen Blaha

All the Megaverse! Starships Exploring the Endless Universes of the Cosmos using the Baryonic Force (Blaha Research, Auburn, NH, 2014)

SuperCivilizations: Civilizations as Superorganisms (McMann-Fisher Publishing, Auburn, NH, 2010)

All the Universe! Faster Than Light Tachyon Quark Starships & Particle Accelerators with the LHC as a Prototype Starship Drive Scientific Edition (Pingree-Hill Publishing, Auburn, NH, 2011).

Unification of God Theory and Unified SuperStandard Model THIRD EDITION (Pingree Hill Publishing, Auburn, NH, 2018).

The Exact QED Calculation of the Fine Structure Constant Implies ALL 4D Universes have the Same Physics/Life Prospects (Pingree Hill Publishing, Auburn, NH, 2019).

Unified SuperStandard Theory and the SuperUniverse Model: The Foundation of Science (Pingree Hill Publishing, Auburn, NH, 2018).

Quaternion Unified SuperStandard Theory (The QUeST) and Megaverse Octonion SuperStandard Theory (MOST) (Pingree Hill Publishing, Auburn, NH, 2020).

Unified SuperStandard Theories for Quaternion Universes & The Octonion Megaverse (Pingree Hill Publishing, Auburn, NH, 2020).

The Essence of Eternity: Quaternion & Octonion SuperStandard Theories (Pingree Hill Publishing, Auburn, NH, 2020).

Available on Amazon.com, bn.com Amazon.co.uk and other international web sites as well as at better bookstores (through Ingram Distributors).

CONTENTS

INTRODUCTION 1

1. DIMENSIONS OF UNIFIED SUPERSTANDARD THEORIES 3
   1.1 QUeST Dimensions 3
   1.2 Breakup of QUeST Space into Space-time and Internal Symmetry Groups 6
   1.3 Justification for a Four Layer QUeST 7
   1.4 One Layer QUeST Structure 7
   1.5 Four Layer QUeST 8
   1.6 Particles of UST and QUeST 10
   1.7 QUeST Vector Bosons 10

2. MEGAVERSE 32 COMPLEX OCTONION SPACE (MOST) 13
   2.1 One Layer MOST 15
   2.2 Four Layer MOST 16
   2.3 Justification for a Four Layer MOST 17
   2.4 Fermion and Gauge Vector Boson Spectrums 17

3. PARTICLE-DIMENSION DUALITY 19
   3.1 Particle-Dimension Duality in our QUeST Universe 19
   3.2 Particle-Dimension Duality in our MOST Megaverse 21
   3.3 Implications of Particle-Dimension Duality 21

4. STATUS OF ELEMENTARY PARTICLE THEORY 23
   4.1 Unified SuperStandard Theory (UST) 23
   4.2 Quaternion Unified SuperStandard Theory (QUeST) 24
   4.3 Potential QUeST Perturbation Theory Divergences 24
   4.4 Consequences 25
   4.5 MOST Extension to the Megaverse/Multiverse 25
   4.6 Future Directions 25

5. PARTICLE FUNCTIONALS 27
   5.1 Quantum Entanglement and Action-at-a-Distance 27
   5.2 Functional Factorization of Quantum Fields 27
   5.3 Motivation for Quantum Field Factorization: Instantaneous Effects in Quantum
   Phenomena 28
   5.4 General Form of Factorization 28
   5.5 Factorization of Fermion Quantum Fields 29
   5.6 The EPR Two System State Example 29
   5.7 Factorization Details 30

6. FUNCTIONALS IN QUEST'S 32 DIMENSION COMPLEX QUATERNION SPACE 32
6.1 Form of a Fundamental Fermion Particle Functional 32
6.2 Particle Functional Byte Numbering 33

7. PARTICLE FUNCTIONALS FEATURES 34
7.1 The Logic Core of Fundamental Fermions and Bosons 34
7.1.1 The Logic Building Block of Fermions – Qube Cores 34
7.1.2 Mass of a Qube 35
7.2 Quba Cores of Fundamental Bosons 37
7.3 Particle Functional Space 37
7.4 Wave Space 37
7.5 Skeleton Functional Lagrangians 38
7.6 Functional Interactions and Feynman Diagrams 39
7.7 Functional Space and Feynman Path Integrals 39
7.8 Functional Space and Feynman Path Integrals 40

8. COMPUTATIONAL LANGUAGE INTERPRETATION OF PARTICLE FUNCTIONAL TRANSFORMATIONS 41
8.1 Languages and Grammars 41
8.2 Example of Production Rules 42
8.3 Example of the Production Rules for a Lagrangian Interaction Term 43
8.4 Particle Functional Transformations Identified as Production Rules 44

9. MONADS, OBSERVABILITY, CONSCIOUSNESS 47
9.1 Observability 47
9.2 Absolute Reality 48
9.3 Relation to Consciousness 48
9.4 The Spark of Monads 49

10. THE QUESTION OF CONSCIOUSNESS 51
10.1 A 19th Century Level 51
10.2 Types of Consciousness SUSCEPTIBLE TO TESTING 51
10.3 Tests for Intrinsic and Inventive Consciousness 52

11. AN INTRINSIC/INVENTIVE CONSCIOUS UNIVERSE 54
11.1 Consciousness and the Universe 54
11.2 Mechanics of Consciousness 54
11.3 The Consciousness Platform 54
11.4 Dynamic Processing 55
11.5 Consciousness in the Universe 55

12. A VERY CONSCIOUS UNIVERSE 57

REFERENCES 59
INDEX 69
ABOUT THE AUTHOR 72

FIGURES and TABLES

Figure 1.1. Psiphi diagram of the dimensions of 8 dimension complex quaternion space. Each row represents a complex quaternion with 8 dimensions. 4

Figure 1.2. Psiphi diagram of the dimensions of 32 dimension complex quaternion space. Each row again represents a complex quaternion with 8 dimensions. 4

Figure 1.3. Psiphi diagram showing partitioning of 8 dimension complex quaternion space. The blocks of dimensions yield 4 complex dimension space-time, and the internal symmetries of normal matter and Dark matter $SU(2)\otimes U(1)\otimes SU(3)\otimes U(2)\otimes SU(2)\otimes U(1)\otimes SU(3)\otimes U(2)$ as they appear in UST. The lower U(4) groups are for the Generation group and the Layer group for normal matter and for Dark matter in one layer UST. The U(2) group transforms between normal and Dark matter. 6

Figure 1.4. Schematic of the structure of the internal symmetry groups of eq. 1.3 plus 4 complex dimensions space-time. The two large blocks are each 5 dimension complex coordinate representations of $SU(2)\otimes U(1)\otimes SU(3)$. The U(2) group supports transformations (rotations) between normal and Dark matter. 8

Figure 1.5. Four layer QUeST internal symmetry groups and space-time diagram for 32 dimension complex quaternion space. Note the left composite blocks combine to specify a 4 dimension complex quaternion space-time. 9

Figure 1.6. One layer QUeST vector bosons. The four layer QUeST quadruples the above list: with one distinct set for each layer. 10

Figure 1.7. Fermion particle spectrum and partial example of pattern of mass mixing of the Generation, Layer, and Dark grroups. Unshaded parts are the known fermions including an additional, as yet not found, 4th generation shown. The lines on the left side (only shown for one layer) display the Generation mixing within each layer's species. The Generation mixing applies within each layer using a separate Generation group for each layer. The lines on the right side show Layer group mixing with the mixing amongst all four layers for each of the four generations individually. There are four Layer groups. The Dark groups mixing between normal and Dark fermions are shown in the center as horizontal lines. There are 256 fundamental fermions counting quarks as triplets. 12

Figure 2.1. Eight-Dimensional (7 + 1) complex octonion subspace with coordinates represented by • 's. This subspace has 128 real dimensions. 13

Figure 2.2. Schematic of the internal symmetry groups' dimensions of Fig. 2.1. The two "large" blocks are each sets of 20 real dimensions furnishing representations of the indicated groups. The lower U(4) groups are the Generation and Layer number groups. The Dark U(4) group is shown. The total number of real dimensions is 112. 14

Figure 2.3. Schematic of the internal symmetry groups of eq. 2.1 including the Dark U(4) group. These are the internal symmetry groups of one layer MOST. The lower U(4) groups above are the Generation and Layer number groups. One pair of each number group is for each of the four U(1)⊗SU(2)⊗SU(3) factors above. 15

Figure 2.4. One layer MOST vector bosons list from eq. 2.1. The four layer MOST quadruples the above list: with one distinct set for each layer. In one layer the total number of vector bosons of the above list is 192. Thus four layers yield a total count of 768 vector bosons in MOST (not counting the Species group which comes from General Relativity). We require each layer has a separate Dark U(4) rotation group. ... 16

Figure 2.5. The 32 dimension MOST schematic. Four layer MOST has 512 real dimensions. 16

Figure 2.6. Schematic spectrum of the fermions of 4 layer MOST. Each fermion is represented by a •. Quark triplets are represented by a single •. Four sets of four species in four generations which are in turn in 4 layers. Open symbols ○ represent known fermions. There are 512 fundamental fermions taking account of quark triplets. Note the Layer groups determine the layers in UST. **They require 4 layers of 8 complex octonions in Megaverse space leading to the 32 dimension complex octonion space.** 18

Figure 3.1. Schematic spectrum of the fermions of the one layer of normal and Dark fermions matching one layer of 8 rows of complex quaternion space dimensions on a one-to-one basis. The other three layers of space dimensions consisting of 24 complex quaternion dimensions are similar in having a one-to-one correspondence with three UST layers of fermions. UST has a four layer fermion spectrum. They total to 256 dimensions and 256 fundamental fermions. 19

Figure 3.2. Schematic spectrum of the fermions of the one layer of normal and Dark fermions matching one layer of 8 rows of complex octonion space (See Fig. 2.1) on a one-to-one basis. The other three layers of space dimensions consisting of 24 complex octonion dimensions are similar in having a one-to-one correspondence with three UST layers of fermions. UST has a four layer fermion spectrum. They total to 512 dimensions and 512 fundamental fermions. 22

Figure 7.1. Functional Feynman diagram for the above interaction.................................. 39
Figure 11.1. A picture of a computer simulation of connection filaments in the universe. Picture courtesy of Andrew Pontzen and Fabio Governato... 56

INTRODUCTION

In previous books this author has derived the Unified SuperStandard Theory (UST) in our 3 + 1 dimension space-time from Complex General Relativity and Quantum Field Theory suitably extended. We then showed that 32 complex quaternion dimension QUeST gives the identical pattern of Internal Symmetries as UST.

This remarkable coincidence leads us to explore Unified SuperStandard Theories in greater detail.

In this book we examine particle-dimension duality and find that the one-to-one match extends down to the individual fermion and dimension level.

We then develop the monad – particle functional concept that had enabled us to eliminate the issues of instantaneous quantum entanglement with Special Relativity in earlier books.

We also defined a complex octonion space of 32 dimensions called MOST in previous books. It also has a close (fermion) particle-dimension duality.

These considerations led us to consider the implications of monads. We found it provides a basis for a form of conscious universe. The universe has intrinsic consciousness everywhere at the global level. Its dynamics represent a kind of response to stimuli by dynamics without thought. Some neighborhoods in the universe have inventive consciousness—they contain entities having thought processes that can exercise inventiveness.

Thus we find a very conscious universe operating on multiple levels.

The Megaverse also has a close fermion-dimension duality. We find the Megaverse is also very conscious and operates on multiple levels.

1. Dimensions of Unified SuperStandard Theories

Dimensions are usually thought to be static—existing only to be used to define the coordinates of physical theories. They are not thought to have a dynamic aspect. In this chapter we will define the dimensions of the Unified SuperStandard Theory (UST) in our space-time, and in an underlying complex quaternion space that we call QUeST. We will see that the internal symmetries of UST emerge directly from the set of dimensions of QUeST. Thus internal symmetry dimensions of UST and the Standard Model are no longer a subject of mystery and no longer unusual (as they are sometimes portrayed.)

The fundamental UST theory is described in detail in Blaha (2020c) (and earlier books. Its basis in 32 dimension complex quaternion space (QUeST) is described in Blaha (2020d) – also in detail. It is remarkable that QUeST provides an exact fundamental basis for UST.[1]

1.1 QUeST Dimensions

QUeST is defined in a 32 dimension complex quaternion space. There are a total of 256 individual dimensions in this space. In view of the number of dimensions the usual approach of defining coordinates is cumbersome. Consequently we followed a Mathematical Picture Language approach in Blaha (2020d). This approach was originally used by Pythagoras and His School around 500 BCE.[2] Pythagoras used symbols •'s which he called *psiphi* symbols (meaning pebbles).

We will begin with an 8 dimension complex quaternion space which has 64 dimensions. Then we will consider the 32 dimension complex quaternion space which can be viewed as consisting of four layers of 8 dimension complex quaternion space.

---

[1] The basis of UST in QUeST was not known to the author until Fall, 2019 although the form of UST was known to the author many years earlier and recorded in several books.

[2] Kirk (1962) presents much of what is known of the Pythagoreans. This author developed the psiphi diagrams, originally, without being aware of the Pythagorean diagrammatic language.

We express the 8 dimension space as a diagram in Fig. 1.1 It consists of a pattern of psiphi. Then we will partition it into the dimensions of space-time and internal symmetry groups in the next section.

Figure 1.1. Psiphi diagram of the dimensions of 8 dimension complex quaternion space. Each row represents a complex quaternion with 8 dimensions.

Similarly the 32 dimension complex quaternion space is depicted as in Fig. 1.2.

Figure 1.2. Psiphi diagram of the dimensions of 32 dimension complex quaternion space. Each row again represents a complex quaternion with 8 dimensions.

Fig. 1.1 is a psiphi diagram that represents 7 + 1 coordinates with 8 dimensions:

Time Biquaternion
$$t = (a + ib + jc + kd) + I(a' + ib' + jc' + kd') \qquad (1.1)$$
Spatial Biquaternions
$$x = (a_x + ib_x + jc_x + kd_x) + I(a'_x + ib'_x + jc'_x + kd'_x)$$
$$y = (a_y + ib_y + jc_y + kd_y) + I(a'_y + ib'_y + jc'_y + kd'_y)$$
$$z = (a_z + ib_z + jc_z + kd_z) + I(a'_z + ib'_z + jc'_z + kd'_z)$$
$$x1 = (a_{x1} + ib_{x1} + jc_{x1} + kd_{x1}) + I(a'_{x1} + ib'_{x1} + jc'_{x1} + kd'_{x1})$$
$$y1 = (a_{y1} + ib_{y1} + jc_{y1} + kd_{y1}) + I(a'_{y1} + ib'_{y1} + jc'_{y1} + kd'_{y1})$$
$$z1 = (a_{z1} + ib_{z1} + jc_{z1} + kd_{z1}) + I(a'_{z1} + ib'_{z1} + jc'_{z1} + kd'_{z1})$$
$$w1 = (a_{w1} + ib_{w1} + jc_{w1} + kd_{w1}) + I(a'_{w1} + ib'_{w1} + jc'_{w1} + kd'_{w1})$$

where all coefficients: a, b, c, d, a', b', c', d', and a_i, b_i, c_i, d_i, a'_i, b'_i, c'_i, d'_i for i = x, y, z, w, x1, y1, z1, w1 are *real-valued* numbers, and where I is an additional fundamental quaternion unit that makes each quaternion "complex." Note that the real and imaginary part of each coordinate has the same fundamental quaternion units to permit complex rotations between them.

As we will see we need four iterations of the above set of complex quaternions for the space of QUeST so that it will yield UST upon restriction to real-valued coordinates. Thus QUeST requires a 32 dimension complex quaternion space:

$$t = (a + ib + jc + kd) + I(a' + ib' + jc' + kd') \qquad (1.2)$$
$$x = (a_x + ib_x + jc_x + kd_x) + I(a'_x + ib'_x + jc'_x + kd'_x)$$
$$y = (a_y + ib_y + jc_y + kd_y) + I(a'_y + ib'_y + jc'_y + kd'_y)$$
$$z = (a_z + ib_z + jc_z + kd_z) + I(a'_z + ib'_z + jc'_z + kd'_z)$$
$$x1 = (a_{x1} + ib_{x1} + jc_{x1} + kd_{x1}) + I(a'_{x1} + ib'_{x1} + jc'_{x1} + kd'_{x1})$$
$$y1 = (a_{y1} + ib_{y1} + jc_{y1} + kd_{y1}) + I(a'_{y1} + ib'_{y1} + jc'_{y1} + kd'_{y1})$$
$$z1 = (a_{z1} + ib_{z1} + jc_{z1} + kd_{z1}) + I(a'_{z1} + ib'_{z1} + jc'_{z1} + kd'_{z1})$$
$$w1 = (a_{w1} + ib_{w1} + jc_{w1} + kd_{w1}) + I(a'_{w1} + ib'_{w1} + jc'_{w1} + kd'_{w1})$$
$$\ldots$$
$$w4 = (a_{w4} + ib_{w4} + jc_{w4} + kd_{w4}) + I(a'_{w4} + ib'_{w4} + jc'_{w4} + kd'_{w4})$$

1.2 Breakup of QUeST Space into Space-time and Internal Symmetry Groups

Returning now to psiphi diagrams we find that the 8-dimension complex quaternion space can be partitioned into blocks based on the dimension rules:

U(2) requires 4 dimensions
U(1)⊗SU(2) requires 4 dimensions
SU(3) requires 6 dimensions
U(4) requires 8 dimensions

where the dimensions have real-valued coordinates. Fig. 1.3 shows the partition of one layer QUeST (8 dimensions by eq. 1.1) giving eq. 1.3.

$$SU(2)\otimes U(1)\otimes SU(3)\otimes U(2)\otimes SU(2)\otimes U(1)\otimes SU(3)\otimes U(2) \qquad (1.3)$$

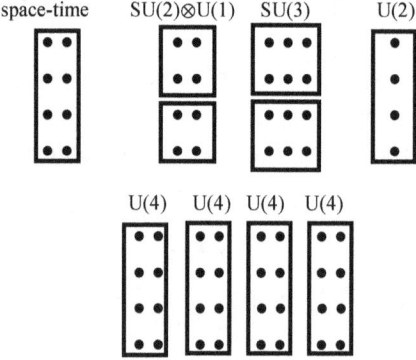

Figure 1.3. Psiphi diagram showing partitioning of 8 dimension complex quaternion space. The blocks of dimensions yield 4 complex dimension space-time, and the internal symmetries of normal matter and Dark matter SU(2)⊗U(1)⊗SU(3)⊗U(2)⊗SU(2)⊗U(1)⊗SU(3)⊗U(2) as they appear in UST. The lower U(4) groups are for the Generation group and the Layer group for normal matter and for Dark matter in one layer UST. The U(2) group transforms between normal and Dark matter.

1.3 Justification for a Four Layer QUeST

There is good reason for QUeST to have four layers embodied in 32 dimension complex quaternion space. If one considers the content of the layer displayed in Fig. 1.3 one sees a 4 dimension complex coordinates block for space-time. To create a 4 dimension complex quaternion coordinates space-time, one needs four layers of the form of Fig. 1.3. *The combination of the four 4-dimension complex coordinate parts is a complex quaternion dimensions space-time.* Thus the choice of four layer QUeST gives us a 4-dimension complex quaternion space-time AND enables QUeST to map directly to UST with its four layers if one limits the quaternion coordinates to the real-valued coordinates within them.[3] If one did not define a four layer QUeST then the role of the four U(4) Layer Groups would be in doubt since the Layer Groups in UST transform among each of the four generations of fermions. (See Fig. 1.6 for an illustration.) Four generations implies a need for four Layer groups, which the 32 complex quaternion QUeST contains. Note four U(2) groups that transform between normal and Dark sectors for each layer are required. We call these groups *Dark* groups.

We conclude four layer QUeST is needed to have a 4 dimension complex quaternion space-time.

1.4 One Layer QUeST Structure

As a preliminary to four layer 32 complex quaternion dimensions QUeST we display the structure implicit in Fig. 1.3 in Fig. 1.4.

---

[3] The Layer groups of UST enable mixing between the layers of fermions as shown in Fig. 2.1.

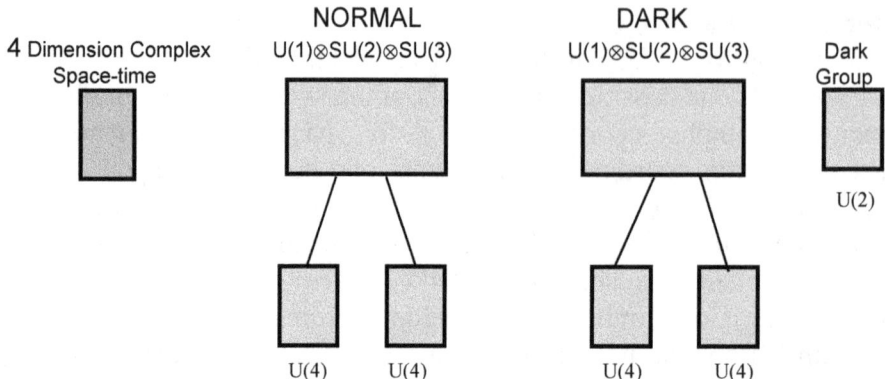

Figure 1.4. Schematic of the structure of the internal symmetry groups of eq. 1.3 plus 4 complex dimensions space-time. The two large blocks are each 5 dimension complex coordinate representations of $SU(2) \otimes U(1) \otimes SU(3)$. The U(2) group supports transformations (rotations) between normal and Dark matter.

1.5 Four Layer QUeST

Fig. 1.5 shows four layer QUeST internal symmetry groups and 4 dimension complex quaternion space-time. Fig. 1.7 shows the 4 layer fundamental fermion spectrum. Fig. 3.1 shows the map between 32 dimension complex quaternion dimensions and fundamental fermions. The map is one-to-one for all four layers.

The 256 dimensions of the 32 dimension complex quaternion space equals the 256 fundamental fermions of QUeST and UST.

The internal symmetry group structure of Fig. 1.5 is

$$[SU(2) \otimes U(1) \otimes SU(3) \otimes SU(2) \otimes U(1) \otimes SU(3) \otimes U(4)^4 \otimes U(2)]^4 \qquad (1.4)$$

plus 4 dimension complex quaternion space-time.

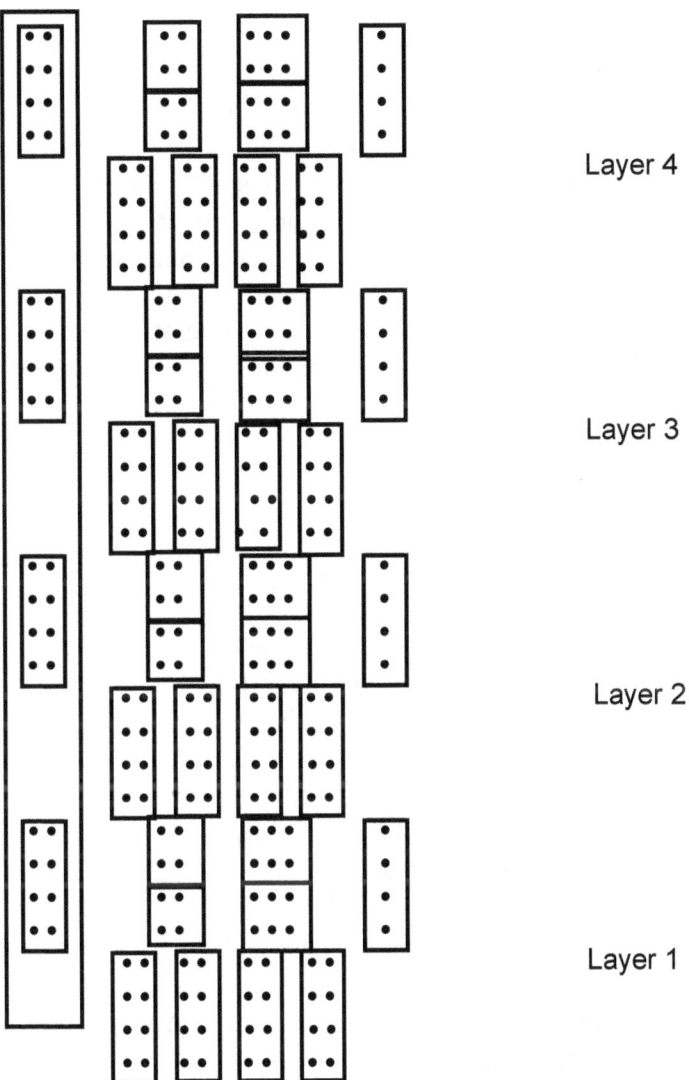

Figure 1.5. Four layer QUeST internal symmetry groups and space-time diagram for 32 dimension complex quaternion space. Note the left composite blocks combine to specify a 4 dimension complex quaternion space-time.

1.6 Particles of UST and QUeST

In Blaha (2020c) and earlier books we found the set of internal symmetry groups of eq. 1.4 to which we added the Dark groups $U(2)^4$ based on a fundamental derivation of UST from QUeST in Blaha (2020a) through (2020c). QUeST provides a fundamental basis for UST and Standard Model internal symmetries removing the questions of strangeness often attributed to Standard Model symmetries.

The fundamental fermions of QUeST were found to be the same as in UST. Fig. 1.7 displays the four layers of fermions of UST and QUeST together with the roles of the Generation groups (vertical within fermion generations), the Layer groups (vertical encompassing all four layers for each generation), and the Dark groups (one-to-one fermion by fermion between normal and Dark sectors). There are 256 fundamental fermions counting quarks as triplets.

1.7 QUeST Vector Bosons

The overall *one layer* QUeST internal symmetry vector bosons are:

"Normal" Gauge Groups
$SU(3) \otimes SU(2) \otimes U(1)$
Generation Group $U(4)$
Layer Group $U(4)$

Dark Gauge Groups
$SU(3) \otimes SU(2) \otimes U(1)$
Generation Group $U(4)$
Layer Group $U(4)$

PLUS

A Dark $U(2)$ group that rotates between the normal and Dark sectors

Figure 1.6. One layer QUeST vector bosons. The four layer QUeST quadruples the above list: with one distinct set for each layer.

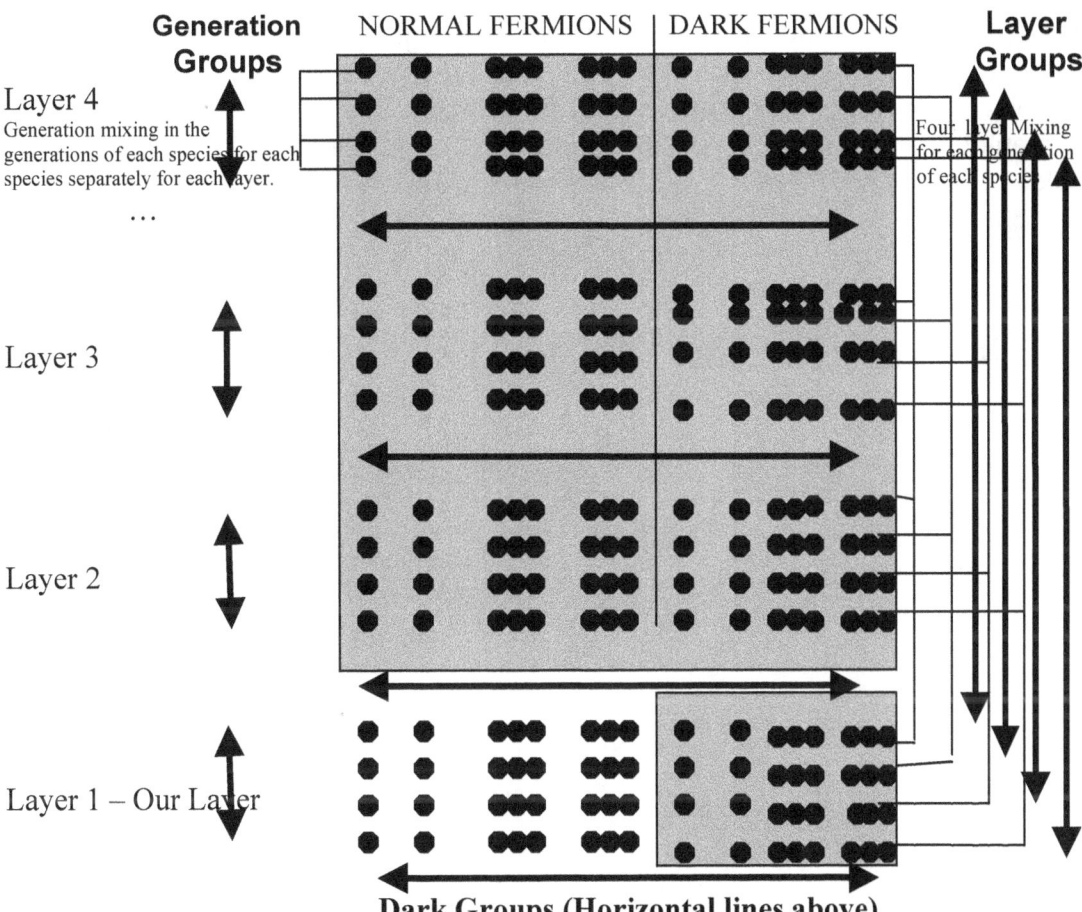

Figure 1.7. Fermion particle spectrum and partial example of pattern of mass mixing of the Generation, Layer, and Dark grroups. Unshaded parts are the known fermions including an additional, as yet not found, 4th generation shown. The lines on the left side (only shown for one layer) display the Generation

mixing within each layer's species. The Generation mixing applies within each layer using a separate Generation group for each layer. The lines on the right side show Layer group mixing with the mixing amongst all four layers for each of the four generations individually. There are four Layer groups. The Dark groups mixing between normal and Dark fermions are shown in the center as horizontal lines. There are 256 fundamental fermions counting quarks as triplets.

2. Megaverse 32 Complex Octonion Space (MOST)

The 32 complex octonion space of the Megaverse (or Multiverse) is factored into a 7 complex quaternion space-time and a set of internal symmetries.[4] The Magaverse can contain our universe as well as a host of other universes.

We find it convenient to split the Megaverse into four 8 complex octonion subspaces. These subspaces are duplicates of each other but contain different internal symmetry groups and different MOST fermion and vector boson spectrums.

Fig 2.1 symbolically depicts an 8-dimension complex octonion space with a psiphi • for each real-valued dimension. *We treat the bioctonion space as a higher dimensional space and do not use details of octonion algebra in our development.*

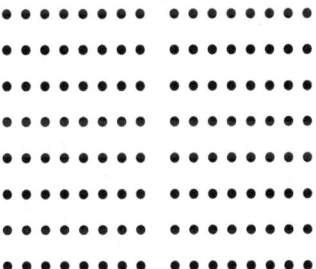

Figure 2.1. Eight-Dimensional (7 + 1) complex octonion subspace with coordinates represented by •'s. This subspace has 128 real dimensions.

The internal symmetry dimensions above number 112. Sixteen of the dimensions serve as the dimensions of an 8-dimension complex space-time. These

---

[4] Much of this chapter appears in Blaha (2020d).

dimensions serve as the fundamental representation dimensions[5] of each of the factors of

$$[SU(2)\otimes U(1)\otimes SU(3)\otimes SU(2)\otimes U(1)\otimes SU(3)]^2 \otimes U(4)^9 \qquad (2.1)$$

counting a U(4) Dark group.

The U(4) Generation and Layer groups are represented in Fig. 2.1. We depict the pattern of symmetry implied by Fig. 2.1 and eq. 2.1 in Fig. 2.2 and 2.3 below.

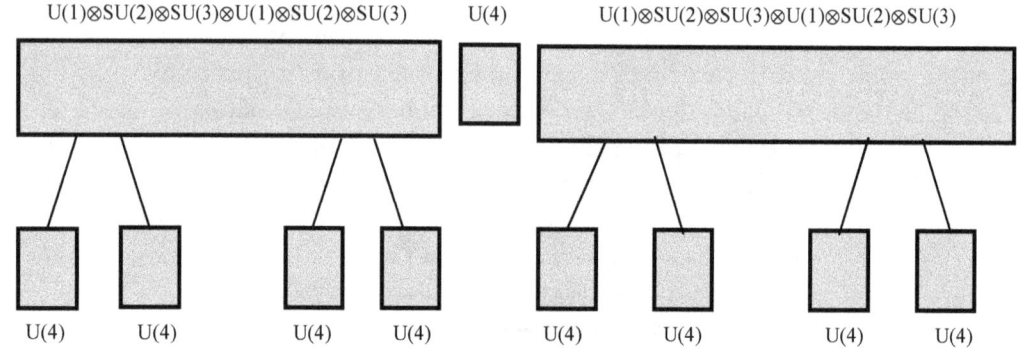

Figure 2.2. Schematic of the internal symmetry groups' dimensions of Fig. 2.1. The two "large" blocks are each sets of 20 real[6] dimensions furnishing representations of the indicated groups. The lower U(4) groups are the Generation and Layer number groups. The Dark U(4) group is shown. The total number of real dimensions is 112.

Each U(1)⊗SU(2)⊗SU(3)⊗U(1)⊗SU(2)⊗SU(3) block in Fig. 2.3 has a 10 complex dimensions (20 real dimensions) representation. The blocks are subdivided in Fig. 2.3 into sets of 10 real dimensions supporting representations of U(1)⊗SU(2)⊗SU(3). We assign the first block to contain the representations of the known parts of the Standard Model. There are three Dark blocks. The internal symmetry groups of each part are listed in Fig. 2.3.

---

[5] See section 1.2.
[6] We also use the term complex dimensions to indicate pairs of rel dimensions.

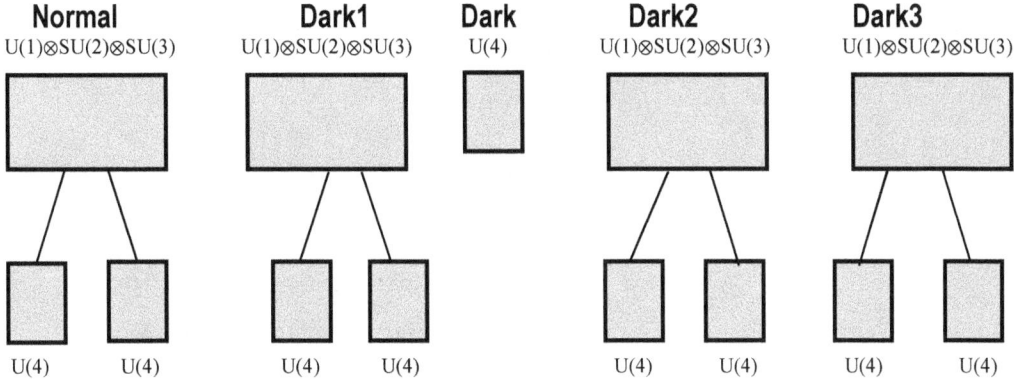

Figure 2.3. Schematic of the internal symmetry groups of eq. 2.1 including the Dark U(4) group. These are the internal symmetry groups of one layer MOST. The lower U(4) groups above are the Generation and Layer number groups. One pair of each number group is for each of the four U(1)⊗SU(2)⊗SU(3) factors above.

2.1 One Layer MOST

The above section specifies the *one layer* MOST. The symmetries of the three other layers are the same but their groups, and fermions, are individual to each layer. The groups of each layer can be flagged with a different index.

The overall one layer MOST internal symmetry is specified by Fig. 2.3, eq. 2.1, and an 8-dimension complex space-time. The internal symmetry groups of one Layer MOST are:

<u>"Normal" Gauge Groups</u>
SU(3)⊗SU(2)⊗U(1)
Generation Group U(4)
Layer Group U(4)
<u>Dark1 Gauge Groups</u>
SU(3)⊗SU(2)⊗U(1)
Generation Group U(4)
Layer Group U(4)

<u>Dark2 Gauge Groups</u>
SU(3)⊗SU(2)⊗U(1)
Generation Group U(4)
Layer Group U(4)

<u>Dark3 Gauge Groups</u>
SU(3)⊗SU(2)⊗U(1)
Generation Group U(4)
Layer Group U(4)

PLUS

A Dark U(4) group that rotates among the four normal and Dark sectors

Figure 2.4. One layer MOST vector bosons list from eq. 2.1. The four layer MOST quadruples the above list: with one distinct set for each layer. In one layer the total number of vector bosons of the above list is 192. Thus four layers yield a total count of 768 vector bosons in MOST (not counting the Species group which comes from General Relativity). We require each layer has a separate Dark U(4) rotation group.

2.2 Four Layer MOST

The four layer MOST is described by a 32 dimension complex octonion space. Thus it consists of four "copies" of the coordinates:

Figure 2.5. The 32 dimension MOST schematic. Four layer MOST has 512 real dimensions.

They yield four duplicates of the internal symmetry schematic in Fig. 2.3, and an 8 complex quaternion space-time consisting of 7 + 1 complex-valued quaternion coordinates (obtained by combining the four layers of 8 dimension complex space-time coordinates.)

The sum total of real dimensions is 512 as is the sum of the dimensions of the above parts constructed from the dimensions.

2.3 Justification for a Four Layer MOST

There is good reason for MOST to have four layers embodied in 32 dimension complex quaternion space. If one considers the content of a layer one sees a 8-dimension complex coordinates block for space-time. To create an 8 dimension complex *quaternion* coordinates space-time, one needs four layers. *The combination of four 8-dimension complex coordinates is an 8 dimension complex quaternion space-time.*

Thus the choice of four layer MOST gives us an 8-dimension complex quaternion space-time that can contain 4-dimension complex quaternion QUeST universes. *We conclude four layer MOST is needed to have an 8-dimension complex quaternion space-time.*

The thirty-two dimension complex octonion space contains an 8-dimension complex quaternion space-time and the four layers of Internal Symmetry groups shown in Fig. 7.5.

2.4 Fermion and Gauge Vector Boson Spectrums

The fermion and vector boson spectrums that emerge in MOST are those of an "enlarged" QUeST and Unified SuperStandard Theory. They are displayed below. MOST has an additional two Dark sectors beyond QUeST and the Unified SuperStandard Theory.

Vector Bosons

From Fig. 2.4 we find MOST has 192 vector bosons in one layer. Thus four layer MOST has a total count of 768 MOST vector bosons. There are two additional Dark vector boson sectors beyond QUeST and the Unified SuperStandard Theory.

Fermions

There are 512 fundamental fermions in MOST, which includes two additional Dark fermion sectors. Fig. 2.6 shows the MOST fermion spectrum.

```
        1       2       3       4
       ••••    ••••    ••••    ••••
       ••••    ••••    ••••    ••••
       ••••    ••••    ••••    ••••
       ••••    ••••    ••••    ••••

       ••••    ••••    ••••    ••••
       ••••    ••••    ••••    ••••
       ••••    ••••    ••••    ••••
       ••••    ••••    ••••    ••••

       ••••    ••••    ••••    ••••
       ••••    ••••    ••••    ••••
       ••••    ••••    ••••    ••••
       ••••    ••••    ••••    ••••

       ••••    ••••    ••••    ••••
       ○○○○    ••••    ••••    ••••
       ○○○○    ••••    ••••    ••••
       ○○○○    ••••    ••••    ••••
```

Figure 2.6. Schematic spectrum of the fermions of 4 layer MOST. Each fermion is represented by a •. Quark triplets are represented by a single •. Four sets of four species in four generations which are in turn in 4 layers. Open symbols ○ represent known fermions. There are 512 fundamental fermions taking account of quark triplets. Note the Layer groups determine the layers in UST. **They require 4 layers of 8 complex octonions in Megaverse space leading to the 32 dimension complex octonion space.**

3. Particle-Dimension Duality

3.1 Particle-Dimension Duality in our QUeST Universe

There is a remarkable correspondence between the dimensions of 32 dimension complex quaternion space and the fermion spectrum of UST and QUeST. Fig. 3.1 shows the map between the dimensions and fermions for one layer (8 complex quaternion dimensions and one layer of fermions in UST.) The other three layers of dimensions and fermions exhibit the same map. Consequently there is a one-to-one correspondence between the 256 dimensions and the 256 fundamental fermions in QUeST.

```
DIMENSIONS                  NORMAL FERMIONS
Real    Imaginary           e   v   up q   down q
••••    ••••                •   •   •••    •••
••••    ••••                •   •   •••    •••
••••    ••••                •   •   •••    •••
••••    ••••                •   •   •••    •••

                            DARK FERMIONS
                            e   v   up q   down q
••••    ••••                •   •   •••    •••
••••    ••••                •   •   •••    •••
••••    ••••                •   •   •••    •••
••••    ••••                •   •   •••    •••
```

Figure 3.1. Schematic spectrum of the fermions of the one layer of normal and Dark fermions matching one layer of 8 rows of complex quaternion space dimensions on a one-to-one basis. The other three layers of space dimensions consisting of 24 complex quaternion dimensions are similar in having a one-to-one correspondence with three UST layers of fermions. UST has a four layer fermion spectrum. They total to 256 dimensions and 256 fundamental fermions.

The map is one-to-one and applies to individual particles and dimensions. Labeling the top row of dimensions of Fig. 3.1 as $d_1, d_2, \ldots, d_8$ we see the duality in detail for the top row of Fig. 3.1:

$$e \leftrightarrow d_1 \qquad (3.1)$$
$$v \leftrightarrow d_2$$
$$q_1 \leftrightarrow d_1 d_4$$
$$q_2 \leftrightarrow d_1 d_5$$
$$q_3 \leftrightarrow d_1 d_6$$
$$q_4 \leftrightarrow d_2 d_4$$
$$q_5 \leftrightarrow d_2 d_5$$
$$q_6 \leftrightarrow d_2 d_6$$

The quarks have both $SU(2) \otimes U(1)$ and $SU(3)$ symmetry resulting in the products of dimensions in the correspondence. (We assume free particles in these discussions.)

The one-to-one map applies to the rows of Fig. 3.1 for both normal and Dark sectors. Fig. 3.1 illustrates the following points:

1. A One-To-One Map: Dimensions – Fermions.

2. The 8 Complex Quaternion Dimensions in each of the top four rows correspond to normal $SU(2) \otimes U(1) \otimes SU(3)$ particles.

3. The 8 Complex Quaternion Dimensions in each of the lower four rows correspond to Dark $SU(2) \otimes U(1) \otimes SU(3)$ particles.

4. The 4 top Complex Quaternion rows corresponding to normal particles implies four fermion generations.

5. The 4 lower Complex Quaternion rows corresponding to Dark particles implies four Dark fermion generations.

6. 4 Layers of 8 Complex Quaternion rows implies 4 layers of fermions as seen in UST.

Thus our QUeST formalism accounts for the number of fermions per generation, the number of generations per layer (4) for normal and Dark fermions, the number of normal and Dark layers (4), the number of space-time dimensions (4), and the number of complex quaternion dimensions[7] (32).

3.2 Particle-Dimension Duality in our MOST Megaverse

There is also a one-to-one correspondence between the dimensions of 32 dimension complex octonion space and the fermion spectrum of MOST. Fig. 3.2 shows the map between the dimensions and fermions for one layer (8 complex octonion dimensions and one layer of fermions in MOST.) The other three layers of dimensions and fermions exhibit the same map. As a result there is a one-to-one correspondence between 512 dimensions and 512 fundamental fermions in MOST – the Unified SuperStandard Theory of the Megaverse.

3.3 Implications of Particle-Dimension Duality

Particle-dimension duality combined with the definition of particle fields in terms of functionals (See Blaha (2020c) and earlier books.), and a map of dimensions to coordinate dimensions of fundamental group representations, and thence to functionals enables us to define a triality of dimensions, functionals and particles. The triality may be symbolized by

$$d_i \leftrightarrow g_i \leftrightarrow f_i$$

where d_i is a dimension, g_i is the dimension taken to be a dimension of a group's fundamental representation, and f_i is a functional which is subject to the group's transformations.

We consider the implications of these considerations in succeeding chapters.

---

[7] Eq. 1.2.

Top Four Rows of One Layer of 8 Complex Octonions

DIMENSIONS	NORMAL FERMIONS
Real Part	e v up q down q
• • • • • • • •	• • • • • • • •
• • • • • • • •	• • • • • • • •
• • • • • • • •	• • • • • • • •
• • • • • • • •	• • • • • • • •
	DARK1 FERMIONS
Imaginary Part	e v up q down q
• • • • • • • •	• • • • • • • •
• • • • • • • •	• • • • • • • •
• • • • • • • •	• • • • • • • •
• • • • • • • •	• • • • • • • •

Lower Four Rows of One Layer of 8 Complex Octonions

DIMENSIONS	DARK2 FERMIONS
Real Part	e v up q down q
• • • • • • • •	• • • • • • • •
• • • • • • • •	• • • • • • • •
• • • • • • • •	• • • • • • • •
• • • • • • • •	• • • • • • • •
	DARK3 FERMIONS
Imaginary Part	e v up q down q
• • • • • • • •	• • • • • • • •
• • • • • • • •	• • • • • • • •
• • • • • • • •	• • • • • • • •
• • • • • • • •	• • • • • • • •

Figure 3.2. Schematic spectrum of the fermions of the one layer of normal and Dark fermions matching one layer of 8 rows of complex octonion space (See Fig. 2.1) on a one-to-one basis. The other three layers of space dimensions consisting of 24 complex octonion dimensions are similar in having a one-to-one correspondence with three UST layers of fermions. UST has a four layer fermion spectrum. They total to 512 dimensions and 512 fundamental fermions.

4. Status of Elementary Particle Theory

Elementary particle theory has gone through a number of phases in the past forty years. Forty years ago model quantum field theories largely based on quantum field theory and various forms of internal symmetries. The motivation for these theories was the success of the Standard Model. It was thought more was needed.

The resulting theories incorporated the Standard Model within generalizations of Standard Model internal symmetries. The primary issue was the justification for proposed internal symmetries.

There was also a deeper approach based on SuperString theory. SuperString theories encountered numerous issues. A primary issue was the selection of a SuperString theory that led inexorably to a physically realistic theory along the lines of the Standard Model. The search for the "true" SuperString theory, if it exists, has occupied the efforts of a sizeable number of theorists for forty years.

In view of the quagmire of theoretic efforts for a Theory of Elementary Particles this author developed a theoretic approach based on a set of fundamental postulates in the manner of Euclid. With six postulates the author was able to develop the known parts in the form of the Standard Model. Part of this development was the introduction of a modified quantum field theory formalism using Two Tier field theory (to eliminate divergences in perturbation theory) and pseudoquantum field theory which supports higher derivative lagrangians in a canonical manner and enables reasonable physics in curved space-times. It also appeared reasonable to base the theory on Complex Special Relativity. Complex General Relativity became necessary in order to create a unified theory for curved space-time. The result was the Unified SuperStandard Theory (UST).

4.1 Unified SuperStandard Theory (UST)

UST had a fundamental fermion spectrum that contained the known fermion spectrum, and added a fourth generation, added four layers of fermions, and added a Dark matter spectrum of fermions that mirrored the normal fermion spectrum. The vector boson interactions contained the ElectroWeak interactions, U(4) interactions that caused interactions between fermions in each layer and similarly for Dark matter. The Generation group interactions yielded $U(4)^8$[8]. The theory also had interactions between the layers of fermions.

UST also contained the Higgs boson sector and gravitational interactions according to a modified General Relativity. General Relativity and the Strong interactions were modified to have higher order derivative field equations. Consequently the gravitational force was modified in a manner similar to MoND. Standard Model interactions were modified to have a linear potential.

The theory is described in Blaha (2018f) and (2020c).

4.2 Quaternion Unified SuperStandard Theory (QUeST)

QUeST was defined in 32 dimension complex quaternion space. The study of QUeST[8] showed that it had the internal symmetries of UST plus an additional Dark U(2) interaction that transformed between normal particles and their Dark equivalents for all four fermion layers giving an additional $U(2)^4$ symmetry.

The space-time generated from QUeST a 4-dimension complex quaternion space that became real 4-dimension space-time in UST when quaternions were restricted to real coordinates.

Thus we saw that UST is properly viewed as derivative from QUeST. This unanticipated result solidified our feeling that QUeST and UST are the true theories of elementary particles.

4.3 Potential QUeST Perturbation Theory Divergences

QUeST is defined in a 4-dimension complex quaternion space-time. Just as 4-dimension complex space-time is restricted to real-valued 4-dimension space-time, QUeST is restricted to the 4-dimension real-valued space-time of UST.

The question then arises of high energy infinities in quaternion space-time since it has 16 real-valued dimensions. Integration in momentum space in this space-time have the general form

$$\int d^{16}k$$

---

[8] See Blaha (2020a) through (2020d)/

Since particle propagators tend to be inverse quadratic (or inverse cubic) it appears that perturbation theory integrations will be highly ultraviolet divergent.

However if one uses Two-Tier coordinates as we do in UST an exponentially convergent factor in all dimensions appears eliminating ultra-violet divergences. In Two-Tier quaternion theory coordinates are replaced with Two-Tier coordinates

$$X^\mu = x^\mu + iY^\mu/M^2$$

for i = 1, 2, ..., 16 where M is a very large mass of the order of the Planck mass presumably. Thus the Two-Tier version of QUeST has convergent perturbation theory integrals.

4.4 Consequences

The smooth transition from QUeST to UST increases the likelihood that QUeST is the true theory of elementary particles and gravitation. It encompasses all we know experimentally. And it has the ability to grow as more is learned about Higgs symmetry breaking.

If QUeST is the correct theory then elementary particle physics become similar to Chemistry. However there is still much to learn about detailed features and much room for the expansion of the understanding of the basis of the theory.

4.5 MOST Extension to the Megaverse/Multiverse

A remarkable aspect of the theoretical approach presented in Blaha (2020c), and here, is its ability to be extended to a Megaverse/Multiverse of universes. MOST showed that a 32 dimension complex octonion space leads to a 8 dimension complex quaternion space-time and an enlarged set of internal symmetries. Thus our universe, and unlimited numbers of additional universes, can "fit" into the MOST Megaverse. The internal symmetries of QUeST are a subset of the internal symmetries of MOST — a salutary feature.. Thus we have a fairly complete total picture of the universe and of the Megaverse.

4.6 Future Directions

Perhaps the most important issue facing particle theory is to obtain an understanding of the rationale for basing QUeST on complex quaternions. We know that Streater (2000) was able to justify extending space-time to complex-valued coordinates. What justification is there for complex quaternion coordinates? The number of these dimensions is 32. A partial justification for 32 dimensions is the need to obtain a 4-dimension complex quaternion space-time from which our real-valued space-time emerges.

Other tasks that remain are:

1. Determine the symmetry breaking for the internal symmetries including the symmetry breakdown(s) of 32 dimension complex quaternion space to internal symmetries and space-time.

2. Find the missing fermions and their interactions.

3. Determine the full set of symmetry breakdown parameters.

4. Find the deeper meaning of Higgs symmetry breaking from vacuum dynamics.

5. Develop a Chemistry of elementary particles.

5. Particle Functionals

5.1 Quantum Entanglement and Action-at-a-Distance

In 1935 Einstein, Podolsky, and Rosen[9] (EPR) raised questions about Quantum Entanglement. EPR considered the quantum entanglement of two systems and showed that instantaneous action-at-a-distance (spookiness) apparently resulted.

In this chapter we show how instantaneity is resolved by "factoring" wave functions into the composition of a functional and a Fourier wave function expansion. in In section 5.3 we show the instantaneity of the EPR two system state example is eliminated using functional factoring of wave functions.

Then we establish a functional formulation of the internal symmetry dimensions of 32 complex quaternion space. The functional formulation then generates fundamental representations of internal symmetry groups.

5.2 Functional Factorization of Quantum Fields

Many years ago Dirac factored the Klein-Gordan equation and obtained the Dirac equation for spin ½ fermions.

In the following sections we show that there is good reason to factor quantum mechanical wave functions and second quantized fields into an inner product of a particle functional and a corresponding Fourier coordinate expansion. With this factorization, and the assumption that the space of all particle functionals, as well as the space of all Fourier coordinate expansions, are both point spaces[10] with the consequence that there is no distance measure in either space, we find a change in one of a pair of space-like separated parts of an initial state causes an instantaneous transformation of the other part (eliminating Einstein's spookiness).

---

[9] Einstein A, Podolsky B, and Rosen N, "Can Quantum-Mechanical Description of Physical Reality Be Considered Complete?", Phys. Rev. **47**, 777 (1935).

[10] The points can be viewed as spaces with no distance measure that are factors in a tensor product with space-time.

5.3 Motivation for Quantum Field Factorization: Instantaneous Effects in Quantum Phenomena

Seemingly instantaneous quantum phenomena are apparent in many cases. For example:

1. Two particles placed in a definite spin state may separate to a space-like distance. If the z component of spin is flipped in one of the particles, the other particle instantaneously flips its spin in such a way as to conserve spin. This type of phenomena has been described as 'spooky' since it violates the law that no effect can travel at a rate faster than the speed of light.

2. Transitions between atomic levels take place instantaneously—in a zero time interval.

Quantum field factorization enables instantaneous effects to happen without violating Relativity.

5.4 General Form of Factorization

Normally fermion and boson quantum fields are described by a wave function of the form

$$\chi(\mathbf{x}, t) \tag{5.1}$$

We can formally factorize quantum fields as an inner product of a functional f_k and a space-time Fourier expansion denoted $(k, \mathbf{x}, t)$ (neglecting internal quantum numbers temporarily) where k is the momentum.

$$\chi(\mathbf{x}, t) = (f_k, (k, \mathbf{x}, t)) \tag{5.2}$$

For a free *two* particle wave function (non-interacting) the wave function may be written as a product of inner products:

$$\chi(\mathbf{x}, t) = (f_{1k}, (k, \mathbf{x}, t)_1)(f_{2q}, (q, \mathbf{x}, t)_2) \tag{5.3}$$

where k and q are momenta.

5.5 Factorization of Fermion Quantum Fields

We now consider the example of a free fermion field to illustrate the general concept. We began by defining a coordinate space Dirac Fourier quantum expansion as

$$(s, x, t) = N(p)[b(p, s)u(p, s)e^{-ip\cdot x} + d^{\dagger}(p, s)v(p, s)e^{+ip\cdot x}] \quad (5.4)$$

where $N(p)$ is a normalization factor, u and v are functions of spin and momentum, and b and $d^{\dagger}$ are creation/annihilation operators. We defined a Dirac quantum wave function with the inner product of a functional and a coordinate space Fourier quantum expansion:

$$\psi(x) = (f, (s, x, t)) = \sum_{\pm s} \int d^3 p N(p)[b(p, s)u(p, s)e^{-ip\cdot x} + d^{\dagger}(p, s)v(p, s)e^{+ip\cdot x}] \quad (5.5)$$

where we use a functional inner product formalism in the manner of Riesz (1955)[11] and others.

5.6 The EPR Two System State Example

EPR considered a state consisting of two systems that might become separated spatially. We can represent the state as

$$\Psi = \sum_n \psi_{1n}(x_1)\psi_{2n}(x_2) \quad (5.6)$$

We can represent a measurement (reduction of state) with a projection Π_{1a} of system "1" to a state ψ_{1a} with

$$\psi_{1a} = \delta_{ab} \Pi_a \psi_{1b} \quad (5.7)$$

Then

$$\Psi_{projected} = \Pi_{1a} \sum_n \psi_{1n}\psi_{2n} = \psi_{1a}(x_1)\psi_{2a}(x_2) \quad (5.8)$$

---

[11] For example see pp. 61-2 of Riesz (1955) where linear functionals and their inner products are defined.

The effect of the measurement of system "1" is *instantaneous* of system "2" because the quantum functionals f_{1n} and f_{2n}, and the projections Π_{1n} and Π_{2n} of both systems are not separated by distance with the result

$$\psi_{1n}(x) = f_{1xn}(\Pi_{1xn}\Phi) = (f_{1xn}, \Pi_{1xn}\Phi) \qquad (5.9)$$
$$\psi_{2n}(y) = f_{2ny}(\Pi_{2yn}\Phi) = (f_{2yn}, \Pi_{2yn}\Phi) \qquad (5.10)$$

with $x = x_1$ and $y = x_2$. *The quantum functional and the projection select the wave and its coordinate parameterization. The coordinates in the wave are merely place holders.*

Therefore the relative distance between the coordinates x_1 and x_2 is not relevant for the change of state of system "2". The quantum functionals and projections give the instantaneity of the change in ψ_{2a} upon the measurement of system "1".

The EPR Spookiness is resolved by quantum functionals. There is no conflict with the Theory of Special Relativity.

5.7 Factorization Details

The rationale for factorization lies in the nature of the functionals and coordinate Fourier expansions that we use. For, we choose to create a space of particle functionals for fermions, bosons, and other particle states that consists of a single point with no distance measure (or alternately put, zero distance between all functionals.) We also choose to create a 'point' space of all coordinate Fourier expansions for bosons and fermions, whose elements have all coordinate values, x.

For the moment we wish to note that the space of functionals includes functionals for all fundamental particles, and all matter/energy composites, in the universe (and the Megaverse). We can describe transitions (interactions) in which functionals are "transformed" into other functionals. So the space of functionals has a dynamic aspect. Another important aspect of functional space is its universality—*all functionals of the Megaverse are present creating a type of link between all parts of the Cosmos*.

The space of coordinate Fourier expansions consists of all possible expansions for particles in the coordinates of each respective universe and of the Megaverse. This space also has no distance measure.

The factorization that we propose enables instantaneous communication of a transition between two space-like separated parts of a state. A change in one part immediately causes a corresponding change in the other part because the changes take place in the functionals which are located at the same point in functional space.

In a certain sense we have divorced quantum phenomena from coordinate space by quantum field factorization.

6. Functionals in QUeST's 32 Dimension Complex Quaternion Space

The dimensions of QUeST space can be initially treated simply as independent dimensions. Dimensions can be mapped to particles and thence to their particle functionals. These functionals can then be used to furnish fundamental representations of internal symmetry groups. They can also be used to define quantum fields for elementary particles as in eq. 3.1. Since some fundamental fermions, namely quarks, have transformation properties of both SU(3) and SU(2)⊗U(1) the quark functionals are equivalent to composites of dimensions. Thus eq. 3.1 becomes

Particle Functional		Dimension Composite	
e	↔	d_1	(6.1)
ν	↔	d_2	
q_1	↔	$d_1 d_4$	
q_2	↔	$d_1 d_5$	
q_3	↔	$d_1 d_6$	
q_4	↔	$d_2 d_4$	
q_5	↔	$d_2 d_5$	
q_6	↔	$d_2 d_6$	

for the SU(3)⊗SU(2)⊗U(1) set of fermions in each generation and each layer of normal and Dark fermions.

6.1 Form of a Fundamental Fermion Particle Functional

The general form of a fermion functional is

$$F_{fermion} = f_{internal} f_{spin} \qquad (6.2)$$

where $f_{internal}$ is labeled with internal symmetry quantum numbers and f_{spin} is labeled by the spin state. They are factored to avoid SU6)-like problems found in the 1960s.

We will call functionals of the form of $F_{fermion}$ *fermion particle functionals*. We will call functionals of the form of $f_{Internal}$ *internal symmetry functionals* since they embody internal symmetries. We will call functionals of the form of f_{spin} *spin functionals* since they embody spin. In chapter 7 we will consider boson functionals.

6.2 Particle Functional Byte Numbering

The 256 fundamental fermions may be numbered from 1 through 256. The ASCII character tables have an 8-bit (byte) numbering. We may then represent a particle functional as

$$f_{byte} = f_{internal} \tag{6.3}$$

using bytes with values from 1 through 256.

Consequently fermions can be characterized as "letters" in an alphabet, and aggregates of fermions can be viewed as words. As a result one may think of the universe as a great Word—a concept which has been put forward many times.[12]

---

[12] A study of this possibility appears in Blaha (1998).

7. Particle Functionals Features

7.1 The Logic Core of Fundamental Fermions and Bosons
In previous books we opened the possibility that fermions (and bosons) might have a core that embodies logic in the form of spin as well as bare masses in the case of fermions. We defined functionals of various spins: 0, ½, 1, and 2. We saw that the core of spin ½ fermion functionals (that we called *qubes* in analogy with *qubits*) have a bare mass that we denoted m_0.

Bosons have cores as well that are boson functionals. Analogously we called a boson core a *quba*[13]. Boson functionals are massless. Bosons acquire masses through interactions.

The rationales for logic cores for particles is discussed in detail in chapters 3 and 8 of Blaha (2018e) and (2020c). We showed that the formalism based on a space of all particle functionals can lead to an explanation of the 'spooky' action at a distance of Quantum Entanglement that has been the subject of much discussion.

7.1.1 The Logic Building Block of Fermions – Qube Cores
If we consider all possible 'things' that might constitute a fundamental building block for a fundamental fermion theory they are all, at best, *ad hoc* and raise questions of their necessity and whether they are composed of yet a more fundamental substructure.

There is only one choice of building block that avoids these issues – a logic unit or qubit. A qubit is a fundamental entity that is a complex form of computer bit. A bit (and thus a qubit) is known to have an energy, or equivalently a mass, and has no

---

[13] We use 'quba' simply because of its similarity to 'qube'. The leading 'b' signifies its bosonic use. We pronounce 'quba' as 'bub' with a silent 'e.' The word 'quba', itself, is the name of a Bantu language spoken by the Bubi people of Bioko Island in Equatorial Guinea.

constituents of a more primitive form.[14] We call a unit of logic that forms the core of a particle a *qube*.[15] It exists as the core of a particle. But, in itself, it has no *independent* material existence or space-time coordinates. A qube is a functional that acquires features such as coordinates, through functional inner products to become an elementary particle. We define a qube as a fermion field theory functional. (See chapters 3 and 8 of Blaha (2018e) or (2020c).)

7.1.2 Mass of a Qube

Recent experiments have shown that a logical value of a qubit has an energy associated with it. One bit of information has about 3×10^{-21} joules of energy[16] or a rest mass, m_0, or about 0.02 eV using $m_0 = E/c^2$. This result was confirmed by E. Lutz et al.[17] who showed that there is a minimum amount of heat produced per bit of erased data. This minimal heat is called the *Landauer*[18] *limit*. The equivalent mass we will call the *Landauer mass* and denote it as m_0. We will assume that a fundamental Landauer mass exists in our discussions although the precise value of the mass will not be used since we may expect all physical particle masses to be renormalized to different values when interactions are taken into account.

We will assume all fermions contain a qube within them. (As stated above bosons do not have qubes within them. We call their core a quba.) A qube is assumed to have mass m_0. The masses of fermions are modified to their known values by interactions.

It is intriguing that the mass of the electron neutrino has been measured in a variety of experiments and found to be within an order of magnitude or so larger than our estimate of the Landauer mass (as we would expect since particles acquire a 'cloud

---

[14] A qube is a physical manifestation of a logical value. The relation of a qube to a logical value is analogous to the relation of a penciled point placed on paper to the concept of a point as a primitive in geometry.

[15] In the Blaha (2018f) we called qubes iotas. However, since the name iota was previously used as a particle name many years ago it seemed reasonable to use a different name. We chose the name 'qube' for self-evident reasons. *'Qube' is pronounced 'cube.'*

[16] E. Muneyuki et al, *Nature Physics*, DOI: 10.1038/NPHYS1821.

[17] E. Lutz et al, Nature **483** (7388): 187–190,10.1038/nature10872, (2012).

[18] R. Landauer, "Irreversibility and heat generation in the computing process", IBM Journal of Research and Development **5** (3): 183–191, (1961).

of virtual particles' due to interactions.) This 'cloud' can be expected to increase its mass above the Landauer mass. Since neutrinos only have the weak interaction it is not surprising that the increase due to interactions should not be large. The Mainz Neutrino Mass Experiment, for example, estimates the electron neutrino mass to be less than 2 eV. The new Karlsruhe Tritium Neutrino Experiment (September, 2019) found an upper limit of less than 1.1 eV.

A number of astronomical studies have also generated estimates of neutrino masses. In July 2010 the 3-D MegaZ DR7 galaxy survey found a limit for the combined mass of the three neutrino varieties to be less than 0.28 eV.[19] A smaller upper bound for the sum of neutrino masses, 0.23 eV, was found in March 2013 by the Planck collaboration,[20] In February 2014 a new estimate of the sum was found to be 0.320 ± 0.081 eV due to discrepancies between the Planck's measurements of the Cosmic Microwave Background, and other predictions, combined with the assumption that neutrinos are the cause of weaker gravitational lensing than implied by massless neutrinos.[21]

Thus the experimentally measured values of neutrino masses are consistent with the qube Landauer mass estimate of 0.02 eV given above. We thus assume that *a fermion particle consists of a qube with a certain mass,[22] which is renormalized, together with other features. These features will emerge later in the derivation of the complete theory.[23]*

We view Reality as ultimately a representation (or painting) of logic values evolving through interactions in time and space.[24]

---

[19] S. Thomas et al, "Upper Bound of 0.28 eV on Neutrino Masses from the Largest Photometric Redshift Survey", Physical Review Letters **105**: 031301 (2010).
[20] Planck Collaboration, arXiv:1303.5076 (2013).
[21] R. A. Battye et al, "Evidence for Massive Neutrinos from Cosmic Microwave Background and Lensing Observations", Phys. Rev. Lett. **112,** 051303 (2014).
[22] Leibniz first proposed the idea of logic 'particles' which he called monads. Our definition of a logic 'particle' does not include (or exclude) the presence of a spiritual part which was part of the definition of Leibniz's monads.
[23] A recent experiment claims to separate the spin part (which we identify as a logical value later) of a molecule from the rest of the molecule.
[24] Those who might suggest matter is substantial, and logic values are not, should remember that matter would be completely insubstantial if there were no forces in nature. Neutrinos which are close to insubstantial would be completely insubstantial if there were no weak interactions.

7.2 Quba Cores of Fundamental Bosons

We defined a corresponding boson functional quba for each type of elementary boson. We designated a boson functional as b_s where s specifies the spin which may be 0, 1, or 2. Every boson contains a boson functional core within it. A quba has the spin of the elementary boson within which it resides. It has zero mass since bosons are typically massless prior to symmetry breaking effects.

An important consequence of the masslessness of qubas is that they have no tachyon equivalents. Note: the bare mass of qubes led to tachyons. The masslessness of qubas prevents Complex Lorentz boosts from generating tachyonic bosons.

7.3 Particle Functional Space

The functionals of elementary particles, form a point space[25] that includes all the free field fermion and boson functionals of our universe and any other universe that might exist (the Megaverse). All fundamental fermions and bosons have a corresponding particle functional. Fermion particle functionals f… are labeled with momentum k, internal symmetry quantum numbers denoted λ, and spin (See eq. 6.2 for the factorized particle functional.) Boson particle functionals b… are similarly labeled with spin s, and internal symmetry quantum numbers.

7.4 Wave Space

We assume the space-time distance between Fourier wave function expansions to be *zero* in keeping with the zero distance between particle functionals in functional space. This assumption is solidly based on the instantaneity of transformations of parts of entangled states. (No spookiness!) Separating the parts of a quantum state S into space-like separated parts S_1 and S_2.we find a change in one part causes an instantaneous change in the other part:

$$<x|S> \rightarrow <x_1|S_1><x_2||S_2> \quad (7.1)$$

irrespective of distance since the implicit functionals and Fourier expansions have no space-time separation from each other.

---

[25] Much of this chapter appears in the Blaha (2018a).

7.5 Skeleton Functional Lagrangians

If we could imagine a 'snapshot' of the universe[26] at one instant of time we could presumably enumerate all the functionals of the universe's particles. Then succeeding snapshots would show an ebb and flow of functionals as time progresses. This thought brings us to the important issue of the transformations of particle functionals in particle interactions. The simplest statement that one could make about functional transformations is that they are created and annihilated according to the interaction terms of the skeletonized Unified SuperStandard Theory (excluding quadratic terms which do not transform functionals.)

We skeletonize a lagrangian density by deleting all quadratic terms and replacing all particle fields by their corresponding functionals.[27] For example the lagrangian

$$\mathcal{L} = \bar{\psi}_C (i\gamma^\mu D_\mu - m)\psi_C(x) + b(\bar{\psi}_C \psi_C(x))^2 \tag{7.2}$$

becomes the skeleton lagrangian

$$\mathcal{L}_S = bf^4 \tag{7.3}$$

where f is the fermion's functional.

Thus our skeletonized lagrangian formalism describes the transitions between functionals in an interaction. This formalism is made more concrete by considering Feynman diagrams for the interactions.

---

[26] We realize that such a snapshot is not possible since infinite velocity particles that could feed a camera this snapshot do not exist.

[27] In our construction of particle functional space we have not introduced complex conjugation of functionals for lack of a good reason. Complex conjugation takes place only in the Fourier expansion part of a quantum field. Another issue is the appearance of lagrangian terms with factors that are derivatives of fields. Since we do not do computations with skeleton lagrangians we can ignore the derivative in each such factor and simply substitute the functional. For example, $\varphi^3(\partial^\mu \varphi)^2$ becomes the quba expression b^5.

7.6 Functional Interactions and Feynman Diagrams

Feynman diagrams with their in and out ordering specify the transformations between functionals more completely. A simple example shows the interaction transformations of functionals. Consider the lagrangian term

$$(\bar{\psi}\psi(x))^2(\partial^\mu\varphi)^2$$

A corresponding Feynman diagram for it is

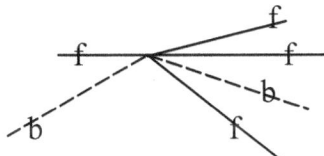

Figure 7.1. Functional Feynman diagram for the above interaction.

with qubes labeled f and qubas labeled b.

When internal symmetries are introduced then the skeletonized lagrangians and the corresponding Feynman diagram representations would be significantly more complicated.

7.7 Functional Space and Feynman Path Integrals

Functionals appear in Feynman Path Integrals and in Faddeev-Popov gauge fixing path integrals. We illustrate the use of functionals in the example:

$$Z(J) = N\int \prod_y dy \; \prod_\varphi d\varphi(y) \; \exp\{i\int d^4y[\mathscr{L}(\varphi(y)) + J^\mu(y)\varphi(y)]\} \quad (7.4)$$

which in functional notational notation becomes

$$Z(J) = N\int \prod_y d(y) \; \prod_b db \; \exp\{i\int d^4y[\mathscr{L}(\varphi(y)) + J^\mu(y)\varphi(y)]\} \quad (7.5)$$

where (y) represents the Fourier expansion in the y coordinates, and with the implied inner product $\varphi(y) = (b, (y))$.

7.8 Functional Space and Feynman Path Integrals

Functionals appear in Feynman Path Integrals and in Faddeev-Popov gauge fixing path integrals. We illustrate the use of functionals in the example:

$$Z(J) = N\int \prod_y dy \prod_\varphi d\varphi(y) \exp\{i\int d^4y[\mathscr{L}(\varphi(y)) + J^\mu(y)\varphi(y)]\} \quad (7.6)$$

which in a functional notational notation becomes

$$Z(J) = N\int \prod_y d(y) \prod_b db \exp\{i\int d^4y[\mathscr{L}(\varphi(y)) + J^\mu(y)\varphi(y)]\} \quad (7.7)$$

where (y) represents the Fourier expansion in the y coordinates, and with the implied inner product $\varphi(y) = (b, (y))$.

8. Computational Language Interpretation of Particle Functional Transformations

In this chapter[28] we will discuss a language interpretation of particle functional transformations based on a Chomsky-like language and grammar. We will see that particle functional transformations can be viewed as grammar production rules with the net result that the evolution of the universe (Megaverse!) can be viewed as the evolution of an enormous Word consisting of a very large but finite number of (terminal) symbols.

8.1 Languages and Grammars

In chapter 3 of Blaha (2005b) we described a linguistic interpretation of particle interactions. In this interpretation particles play the role of symbols (terminal symbols and nonterminal symbols[29]) in an alphabet (of a finite number of symbols) for a Chomsky-like language. Chomsky defines four types of language ranging from type 0 through type 3. Particle theories, when viewed in terms of their perturbation expansions, can be viewed as a generalization of a type 0 language. A type 0 language (also called an unrestricted rewriting system) allows any grammar production rule of the form

$$X \rightarrow Y$$

where X and Y are sets of particles (strings).

---

[28] Most of this chapter appeared in Blaha (2005b) and other books by the author. For more than a hundred years mathematicians and physicists have been describing Physics and Mathematics as being a language in colloquial, layman's terms. Our books show that elementary particle physics, such as our SuperStandard Model, is precisely a type 0 Chomsky language, in which production rules are generated from lagrangian interaction terms. Specific examples are presented in Blaha (2005b) and (2005c).

[29] From a particle view a terminal symbol is a particle that appears in input or output states (strings) of a perturbation theory diagram. A nonterminal symbol is a particle that appears in an intermediate state of a perturbation theory diagram. In the theories that we have considered particles are both terminal and nonterminal symbols.

A production rule is a specification of a transformation of a string of symbols (set of particles) to another string of symbols (set of particles). In the case of quantum theories production rules are inherently quantum probabilistic.

A grammar is specified by a quadruple of items symbolized by the expression

$$<N, T, S, P>$$

where N is a set of nonterminal symbols, T is a set of terminal symbols, S is a special terminal symbol called the head or start symbol, and P is a finite set of production rules. In quantum theories such as the SuperStandard Theory N and T coincide. The start symbol S corresponds to the bare vacuum. Chomsky's definition of a language is the set of all strings of terminal symbols that can be generated from the start symbol using the production rules. *We extend the definition of a particle language to the set of all finite strings of particles (symbols) whether or not they can be generated from the start symbol.*[30]

The set of production rules is finite in Chomsky's definition of language. In the context of quantum field theories we note that a lagrangian of the form of a finite polynomial expression is equivalent to a finite set of production rules.

8.2 Example of Production Rules

In this section we will consider a simple example of production rules with the alphabet:

Start Symbol: S
Nonterminal symbols: A, B
Terminal symbols: x, y

We choose the production rules:

$S \rightarrow AB$ Rule I
$A \rightarrow y$ Rule II

---

[30] If one considers the fact that all particles originate either directly or indirectly from the Big Bang (the Start symbol), then the Chomsky definition of type zero languages applies where all strings originate in the Start symbol of the Big Bang.

$$A \to Ay \quad \text{Rule III}$$
$$B \to x \quad \text{Rule IV}$$
$$B \to Bx \quad \text{Rule V}$$

An example: Generating a string ('particles') yyxxx from the head symbol S using the above production rules:

$$S \to AB$$
$$AB \to AyB$$
$$AyB \to yyB$$
$$yyB \to yyBx$$
$$yyBx \to yyBxx$$
$$yyBxx \to yyxxx$$

8.3 Example of the Production Rules for a Lagrangian Interaction Term

Earlier we noted that a particle lagrangian with a finite number of terms polynomial in particle fields terms would always have a corresponding finite set of production rules. In this section we consider the example of a lagrangian electromagnetic interaction term for electrons and positrons:

$$\overline{e}\gamma \cdot Ae$$

This lagrangian term yields the production rules:

$$e \to eA$$
$$e \to Ae$$
$$eA \to e$$
$$Ae \to e$$
$$p \to pA$$
$$p \to Ap$$

$$pA \to p$$
$$Ap \to p$$
$$ep \to A$$
$$pe \to A$$
$$A \to ep$$
$$A \to pe$$

where e represents an electron, p represents a positron, and A represents the electromagnetic field. Blaha (2005b) presents sequences of transitions using the above production rules and their corresponding Feynman-like diagrams.

Blaha (2005b) also presents other examples such as the ElectroWeak Interaction:

$$\nu_e W^- e$$

where ν_e is an electron type neutrino, and W^- is a negative Weak W vector boson.

8.4 Particle Functional Transformations Identified as Production Rules

Earlier we showed how to define a lagrangian for functionals that provided transformation rules for functionals. In this section we consider the example of a functional lagrangian electromagnetic interaction term for electron and positron functionals:

$$f_e \gamma \cdot b_A f_e$$

This functional lagrangian term yields the functional production rules:

$$f_e \to f_e b_A$$
$$f_e \to b_A f_e$$
$$f_e b_A \to f_e$$
$$b_A f_e \to f_e$$

$$f_p \rightarrow f_p b_A$$
$$f_p p \rightarrow b_A f_p$$
$$f_p b_A \rightarrow f_p$$
$$b_A f_p \rightarrow f_p$$
$$f_e f_p \rightarrow b_A$$
$$f_p f_e \rightarrow b_A$$
$$b_A \rightarrow f_e f_p$$
$$b_A \rightarrow f_p f_e$$

where f_e represents an electron functional, f_p represents a positron functional, and b_A represents the electromagnetic field functional.

9. Monads, Observability, Consciousness

We have seen how particles appear to contain functionals that enable instantaneous quantum entanglement phenomena to take place without conflict with the Theory of Relativity. In this chapter we will see that observability is also directly understood within a monad framework, and that a form of consciousness results.

Individual fundamental fermions and bosons contain functionals that we will call *monads* with certain physical properties. Fermions have qubes; bosons have qubas. We discussed their features earlier. Aggregates of fundamental particles form matter and energy. Thus matter and energy have monads within them.

9.1 Observability

We now turn to the questions of macroscopic observability and quantum observability. At both of these levels of observation monads play a decisive role. At the quantum level we have seen that monads enable instantaneous quantum phenomena to happen without conflict with Special Relativity. Quantum phenomena require observability when measured. *Thus monads, being intimately related to quantum phenomena, may also be viewed as the mechanism for observability at the quantum level.* This feature of monads was discussed in Blaha (2018f) and (2020c). Monads are then the instrument of observability at the quantum level of individual particles.

They are also the instrument of observability at the macroscopic level of aggregates of particles. Being ubiquitous monads answer questions of observability that are frequently posed, which are forms of the question:

Do events take place in the absence of observers?

Answer: YES, because the monads within particles provide a form of "default" level of observation.

9.2 Absolute Reality

Since <u>all</u> monads (functionals) exist in a space with no distance measure there is no question of disparities associated with space-time distances. Thus there is an *absolute reality* from instant to instant—all parts of the universe simultaneously exist *and are in contact with each other in principle*.[31] The universe has a unitary reality with all parts interrelated in the manner that thinkers have hypothesized for thousands of years. (For example: "The universe is one.") The events on a distant star, whose starlight we view, are as real as nearby events on earth. Aggregates of particles, which contain aggregates of monads, unfold dynamically according to physical law.

9.3 Relation to Consciousness

Consciousness has many facets. One facet is the reaction to events. In particle interactions monads transition (in general) to other monads. They do so in accord with quantum theory.

Monads thus have the general feature of reacting to events in a quantum probabilistic manner. They make "decisions" in accord with particle dynamics. Thus they have some features associated with consciousness:

1. Reaction to events

2. Selection of a path from the event point in a quantum probabilistic manner

Monads lack intelligence and decision making capacity beyond quantum dynamics. However many living creatures have similar abilities and limitations. Many creatures react to events according to a genetically determined pattern. One may characterize these creatures as partially conscious. In the next chapter we consider different levels of consciousness. The level of monad consciousness seems to be consistent with the levels of most living creatures. Mankind and other semi-intelligent species will be seen to have a higher level of consciousness.

---

[31] In particular the ubiquitous presence of gravitons—the essence of space-time—provides a universal connection mechanism as we discuss in chapter 11.

9.4 The Spark of Monads

Some thinkers (for example Leibniz) have attributed a spark of consciousness or spirit to monads This property is not determined by physical considerations and will not be considered here..

10. The Question of Consciousness

There are many levels in the study of consciousness. We will consider consciousness at the physical level where it is susceptible to analysis in terms of monads. We will not consider consciousness at the neurophysiological level.

10.1 A 19th Century Level

The eminent alienist (psychiatrist), Bucke,[32] a friend of William James, suggested that there were three levels of consciousness:

Cosmic Consciousness – Its prime characteristic is a consciousness of the Cosmos – the life and order of the rest of the universe. Possessed by some individuals in Bucke's view.

Self Consciousness – Conscious of surroundings as well as being self aware and aware of being conscious and distinct from the rest of the universe. Possessed by Mankind and higher animals such as primates.

Simple Consciousness – Conscious of nearby things and conscious of parts of itself. Possessed by half of the animal kingdom, and now viewed as applying to lower orders as well.

In chapter 11 we suggest the universe is "living" with non-conscious parts and having simple consciousness.

10.2 Types of Consciousness SUSCEPTIBLE TO TESTING

Bucke's, and many other views of consciousness, are not easily, and convincingly, testable. Our characterization of the types of consciousness differentiates

---

[32] See Bucke (1901). His book was highly thought of by William James among others.

between intrinsic (genetically-based or equivalent) consciousness and inventive consciousness (based on thought and consideration of alternatives in situations).

1. Intrinsic Consciousness

   All living creatures have an ability to detect a situation and generally to react to it in some way. Those creatures whose reaction mechanism is solely specified genetically (or by some dynamical program) almost always react in the same way to a given situation. Their genes/dynamics specify it. If a creature is totally governed by its genetics (or an equivalent dynamics) then we say it has *intrinsic consciousness*. One can view lifeless aggregates of matter as having intrinsic consciousness since they have well-defined physical properties with an inherent dynamics that serves to determine their behavior in situations. The universe because of its contents may also be viewed as having intrinsic consciousness. (We explore this case in more detail later.)

2. Inventive Consciousness

   Those creatures that have genetically based consciousness, but also go beyond their genetics in various situations to react based on thoughtful consideration of alternatives, have *inventive consciousness*. They execute responses based on thought. The process of thought may (and probably is) based on a genetically (or dynamically) based platform for thought. This form of consciousness involves the inventive consideration of alternatives and an assessment of the relative probabilities of success.

10.3 Tests for Intrinsic and Inventive Consciousness

Many studies of consciousness propose mechanisms and structures for consciousness. They often don't suggest definitive tests for their characterizations. In our specification of types of consciousness there is a clear distinguishing test:

If a creature gives the same response to an event for any number of tries with modest variations in the event and response, then the response characterizes intrinsic consciousness. If this pattern is true for the creature for all events, then its intrinsic consciousness in confirmed.

On the other hand if a creature has varying responses to a series of similar events, then the creature is displaying inventive consciousness.

In the case of inanimate objects the test simply becomes an analysis of the dynamic cause of the responses of the object.

From the previous chapter we see monads exhibit intrinsic consciousness. They have a behavior determined by their dynamics. However, if one has a large aggregate of monads, which are, after all, quantum probabilistic, then it is possible for a sufficiently large, and "carefully" constructed, aggregate to exhibit inventive consciousness.

11. An Intrinsic/Inventive Conscious Universe

11.1 Consciousness and the Universe

We have seen that particles contain monads that enable instantaneous quantum entanglement phenomena to take place without conflict with the Theory of Relativity. Monads contain some of the features of consciousness—particularly quantum and macroscopic observability.

11.2 Mechanics of Consciousness

While a computer metaphor does not adequately characterize the range of conscious activity, it has the advantage of providing a framework for the general analysis of consciousness. For that reason we consider a computer-like model of consciousness.

We can view consciousness (and intelligence) as based on an adequate platform and a set of instructions (including the capability to be inventive) that govern the behavior of an entity.

11.3 The Consciousness Platform

The platform for living entities has a size issue and a complexity issue. As we see in the particular case of primates the size of the brain[33] (in this case) seems to be directly correlated with the level of consciousness and the level of intelligence. Smaller brain size indicates a lower level of intelligence and consciousness when we compare primate species.

There is also a perceived limit to brain size—a size significantly larger than that of the human brain leads to transmission issues. The exchange of information between

---

[33] We will discuss the platform issues in terms of brains. One could frame the discussion in terms of a "blob" of matter.

the parts of the brain, which is critical for coherent consciousness, is limited by neural transmission speeds.

A part of this discussion presupposes a sufficiently complex structure within the brain. Living creatures have a wonderfully intricate, extremely compact, brain structure.

In the case of non-living entities we can frame the discussion in terms of a computer memory. Again the issues of size and complexity come to the forefront. An example is the type of supercomputers, which use complex structure, compactness, and extremely low temperatures to perform activities somewhat resembling consciousness.

11.4 Dynamic Processing

The mechanisms of the platform require a processor to perform intellectual and consciousness activities. In the case of non-living entities the processor may be deterministic, or classical or quantum probabilistic. Processing can be specified by "computer software" or dynamically through classical or quantum theories. An important part of processing (and consequently consciousness) is the ability of the processor to dynamically refigure itself. We call that procedure learning.

For living organisms the processing is embedded within the brain genetically or through environmental/social conditioning. Consciousness is embedded within the processor in the brain. The level of consciousness (and intelligence) is determined by the capacity of the platform and the content of the processor. A particularly important aspect is the input/output channels available to the processor. The inputs are typically from the senses. The outputs are directives issued to bodily organs.

11.5 Consciousness in the Universe

Monads give breadth to the universe expanding its intrinsic consciousness; monad diversity gives a bigger platform Perhaps the most important aspect of consciousness is the connectivity of the parts.

On the micro-level the monads of gravitons is the greatest source of connectivity due to their ubiquitous presence in infinite quantity at every point of space-time. The vacuum also is a major part of connectivity.

The next level of connectivity is particles of matter and energy: fermions, bosons, Higgs Particles and so on.

Aggregates of matter and energy also support connectivity: planets, stars, galaxies, filaments, super galaxies, black holes, and worm holes (if they exist).

The filaments seen between galaxies vividly display connectivity. See Fig. 11.1 for an illustrative example.

Overall we see enormous interconnectivity in the universe. The space between clumps of matter and energy has intrinsic consciousness based on the laws of physics. Within the clumps of matter and energy there are sites of inventive consciousness. We know of one site, earth. But other sites most likely exist and may contain living or non-living entities with inventive consciousness.

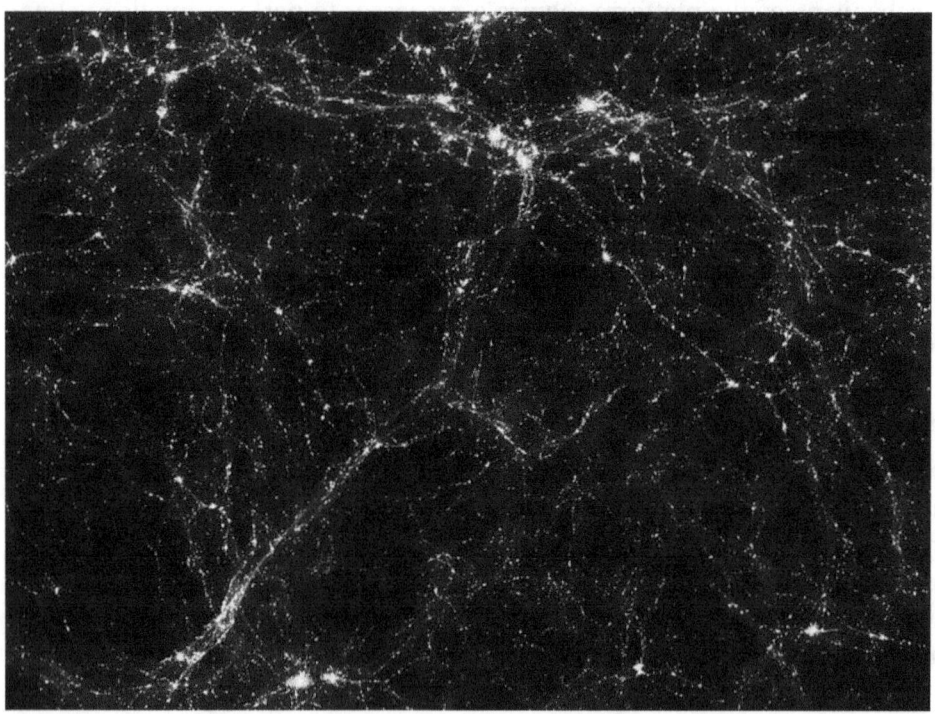

Figure 11.1. A picture of a computer simulation of connection filaments in the universe. Picture courtesy of Andrew Pontzen and Fabio Governato.

12. A Very Conscious Universe

The universe is an unexcelled platform for a type of consciousness. We have found the contents of the universe to support monad-based consciousness on two levels: the intrinsic level through the laws of physics and their dynamics, and the inventive level through the entities with a higher level of internal organization supporting inventive thought.

The universe combines an extremely large platform (gravitation, the planets, stars, galaxies and so on) with instantaneous communication (connectivity) through particle functionals (monads). The result is a very conscious universe operating on multiple levels.

The Megaverse also has a close fermion-dimension duality. A similar discussion and conclusion applies to it. The Megaverse is also very conscious and operates on multiple levels.

REFERENCES

Akhiezer, N. I., Frink, A. H. (tr), 1962, *The Calculus of Variations* (Blaisdell Publishing, New York, 1962).

Bjorken, J. D., Drell, S. D., 1964, *Relativistic Quantum Mechanics* (McGraw-Hill, New York, 1965).

Bjorken, J. D., Drell, S. D., 1965, *Relativistic Quantum Fields* (McGraw-Hill, New York, 1965).

Blaha, S., 1998, *Cosmos and Consciousness* (Pingree-Hill Publishing, Auburn, NH, 1998).

_____, 2002, *A Finite Unified Quantum Field Theory of the Elementary Particle Standard Model and Quantum Gravity Based on New Quantum Dimensions™ & a New Paradigm in the Calculus of Variations* (Pingree-Hill Publishing, Auburn, NH, 2002).

_____, 2003, *A Finite Unified Quantum Field Theory of the Elementary Particle Standard Model and Quantum Gravity Based on New Quantum Dimensions™ and a New Paradigm in the Calculus of Variations* (Pingree-Hill Publishing, Auburn, NH, 2003).

_____, 2004, *Quantum Big Bang Cosmology: Complex Space-time General Relativity, Quantum Coordinates™ Dodecahedral Universe, Inflation, and New Spin 0, ½, 1 & 2 Tachyons & Imagyons* (Pingree-Hill Publishing, Auburn, NH, 2004).

_____, 2005a, *Quantum Theory of the Third Kind: A New Type of Divergence-free Quantum Field Theory Supporting a Unified Standard Model of Elementary Particles and Quantum Gravity based on a New Method in the Calculus of Variations* (Pingree-Hill Publishing, Auburn, NH, 2005).

_____, 2005b, *The Metatheory of Physics Theories, and the Theory of Everything as a Quantum Computer Language* (Pingree-Hill Publishing, Auburn, NH, 2005).

_____, 2005c, *The Equivalence of Elementary Particle Theories and Computer Languages: Quantum Computers, Turing Machines, Standard Model, Superstring Theory, and a Proof that Gödel's Theorem Implies Nature Must Be Quantum* (Pingree-Hill Publishing, Auburn, NH, 2005).

_____, 2006a, *The Foundation of the Forces of Nature* (Pingree-Hill Publishing, Auburn, NH, 2006).

_____, 2006b, *A Derivation of ElectroWeak Theory based on an Extension of Special Relativity; Black Hole Tachyons; & Tachyons of Any Spin.* (Pingree-Hill Publishing, Auburn, NH, 2006).

_____, 2007a, *Physics Beyond the Light Barrier: The Source of Parity Violation, Tachyons, and A Derivation of Standard Model Features* (Pingree-Hill Publishing, Auburn, NH, 2007).

_____, 2007b, *The Origin of the Standard Model: The Genesis of Four Quark and Lepton Species, Parity Violation, the ElectroWeak Sector, Color SU(3), Three Visible Generations of Fermions, and One Generation of Dark Matter with Dark Energy* (Pingree-Hill Publishing, Auburn, NH, 2007).

_____, 2008a, *A Direct Derivation of the Form of the Standard Model From GL(16)* (Pingree-Hill Publishing, Auburn, NH, 2008).

_____, 2008b, *A Complete Derivation of the Form of the Standard Model With a New Method to Generate Particle Masses Second Edition* (Pingree-Hill Publishing, Auburn, NH, 2008)

_____, 2009, *The Algebra of Thought & Reality: The Mathematical Basis for Plato's Theory of Ideas, and Reality Extended to Include A Priori Observers and Space-Time Second Edition* (Pingree-Hill Publishing, Auburn, NH, 2009).

_____, 2010a, *Operator Metaphysics: A New Metaphysics Based on a New Operator Logic and a New Quantum Operator Logic that Lead to a Mathematical Basis for Plato's Theory of Ideas and Reality* (Pingree-Hill Publishing, Auburn, NH, 2010).

_____, 2010b, *The Standard Model's Form Derived from Operator Logic, Superluminal Transformations and GL(16)* (Pingree-Hill Publishing, Auburn, NH, 2010).

_____, 2010c, *SuperCivilizations: Civilizations as Superorganisms* (McMann-Fisher Publishing, Auburn, NH, 2010).

_____, 2011a, *21st Century Natural Philosophy Of Ultimate Physical Reality* (McMann-Fisher Publishing, Auburn, NH, 2011).

_____, 2011b, *All the Universe! Faster Than Light Tachyon Quark Starships & Particle Accelerators with the LHC as a Prototype Starship Drive Scientific Edition* (Pingree-Hill Publishing, Auburn, NH, 2011).

_____, 2011c, *From Asynchronous Logic to The Standard Model to Superflight to the Stars* (Blaha Research, Auburn, NH, 2011).

_____, 2012a, *From Asynchronous Logic to The Standard Model to Superflight to the Stars volume 2: Superluminal CP and CPT, U(4) Complex General Relativity and The Standard Model, Complex Vierbein General Relativity, Kinetic Theory, Thermodynamics* (Blaha Research, Auburn, NH, 2012).

_____, 2012b, *Standard Model Symmetries, And Four And Sixteen Dimension Complex Relativity; The Origin Of Higgs Mass Terms* (Blaha Reasearch, Auburn, NH, 2012).

_____, 2013a, *Multi-Stage Space Guns, Micro-Pulse Nuclear Rockets, and Faster-Than-Light Quark-Gluon Ion Drive Starships* (Blaha Research, Auburn, NH, 2013).

_____, 2013b, *The Bridge to Dark Matter; A New Sister Universe; Dark Energy; Inflatons; Quantum Big Bang; Superluminal Physics; An Extended Standard Model Based on Geometry* (Blaha Reasearch, Auburn, NH, 2013).

_____, 2014a, *Universes and Megaverses: From a New Standard Model to a Physical Megaverse; The Big Bang; Our Sister Universe's Wormhole; Origin of the Cosmological Constant, Spatial Asymmetry of the Universe, and its Web of Galaxies; A Baryonic Field* between Universes and Particles; Megaverse Extended Wheeler-DeWitt Equation* (Blaha Reasearch, Auburn, NH, 2014).

_____, 2014b, *All the Megaverse! Starships Exploring the Endless Universes of the Cosmos Using the Baryonic Force* (Blaha Research, Auburn, NH, 2014).

_____, 2014c, *All the Megaverse! II Between Megaverse Universes: Quantum Entanglement Explained by the Megaverse Coherent Baryonic Radiation Devices – PHASERs Neutron Star Megaverse Slingshot Dynamics Spiritual and UFO Events, and the Megaverse Microscopic Entry into the Megaverse* (Blaha Research, Auburn, NH, 2014).

_____, 2015a, *PHYSICS IS LOGIC PAINTED ON THE VOID: Origin of Bare Masses and The Standard Model in Logic, U(4) Origin of the Generations, Normal and Dark Baryonic Forces, Dark Matter, Dark Energy, The Big Bang, Complex General Relativity, A Megaverse of Universe Particles* (Blaha Research, Auburn, NH, 2015).

_____, 2015b, *PHYSICS IS LOGIC Part II: The Theory of Everything, The Megaverse Theory of Everything, U(4)⊗U(4) Grand Unified Theory (GUT), Inertial Mass = Gravitational Mass, Unified Extended Standard Model and a New Complex General Relativity with Higgs Particles, Generation Group Higgs Particles* (Blaha Research, Auburn, NH, 2015).

_____, 2015c, *The Origin of Higgs ("God") Particles and the Higgs Mechanism: Physics is Logic III, Beyond Higgs – A Revamped Theory With a Local Arrow of Time, The Theory of Everything Enhanced, Why Inertial Frames are Special, Universes of the Mind* (Blaha Research, Auburn, NH, 2015).

_____, 2015d, *The Origin of the Eight Coupling Constants of The Theory of Everything: U(8) Grand Unified Theory of Everything (GUTE), S^8 Coupling Constant Symmetry, Space-Time Dependent Coupling Constants, Big Bang Vacuum Coupling Constants, Physics is Logic IV* (Blaha Research, Auburn, NH, 2015).

_____, 2016a, *New Types of Dark Matter, Big Bang Equipartition, and A New U(4) Symmetry in the Theory of Everything: Equipartition Principle for Fermions, Matter is 83.33% Dark,*

Penetrating the Veil of the Big Bang, Explicit QFT Quark Confinement and Charmonium, Physics is Logic V (Blaha Research, Auburn, NH, 2016).

_____, 2016b, *The Periodic Table of the 192 Quarks and Leptons in The Theory of Everything: The U(4) Layer Group, Physics is Logic VI* (Blaha Research, Auburn, NH, 2016).

_____, 2016c, *New Boson Quantum Field Theory, Dark Matter Dynamics, Dark Matter Fermion Layer Mixing, Genesis of Higgs Particles, New Layer Higgs Masses, Higgs Coupling Constants, Non-Abelian Higgs Gauge Fields, Physics is Logic VII* (Blaha Research, Auburn, NH, 2016).

_____, 2016d, *Unification of the Strong Interactions and Gravitation: Quark Confinement Linked to Modified Short-Distance Gravity; Physics is Logic VIII* (Blaha Research, Auburn, NH, 2016).

_____, 2016e, *MoND: Unification of the Strong Interactions and Gravitation II, Quark Confinement Linked to Large-Scale Gravity, Physics is Logic IX* (Blaha Research, Auburn, NH, 2016).

_____, 2016f, *CQ Mechanics: A Unification of Quantum & Classical Mechanics, Quantum/Semi-Classical Entanglement, Quantum/Classical Path Integrals, Quantum/Classical Chaos* (Blaha Research, Auburn, NH, 2016).

_____, 2016g, *GEMS: Unified Gravity, ElectroMagnetic and Strong Interactions: Manifest Quark Confinement, A Solution for the Proton Spin Puzzle, Modified Gravity on the Galactic Scale* (Pingree Hill Publishing, Auburn, NH, 2016).

_____, 2016h, *Unification of the Seven Boson Interactions based on the Riemann-Christoffel Curvature Tensor* (Pingree Hill Publishing, Auburn, NH, 2016).

_____, 2017a, *Unification of the Eleven Boson Interactions based on 'Rotations of Interactions'* (Pingree Hill Publishing, Auburn, NH, 2017).

_____, 2017b, *The Origin of Fermions and Bosons, and Their Unification* (Pingree Hill Publishing, Auburn, NH, 2017).

_____, 2017c, *Megaverse: The Universe of Universes* (Pingree Hill Publishing, Auburn, NH, 2017).

_____, 2017d, *SuperSymmetry and the Unified SuperStandard Model* (Pingree Hill Publishing, Auburn, NH, 2017).

_____, 2017e, *From Qubits to the Unified SuperStandard Model with Embedded SuperStrings: A Derivation* (Pingree Hill Publishing, Auburn, NH, 2017).

_____, 2017f, *The Unified SuperStandard Model in Our Universe and the Megaverse: Quarks, ... ,* (Pingree Hill Publishing, Auburn, NH, 2017).

_____, 2018a, *The Unified SuperStandard Model and the Megaverse SECOND EDITION A Deeper Theory based on a New Particle Functional Space that Explicates Quantum Entanglement Spookiness (Volume 1)* (Pingree Hill Publishing, Auburn, NH, 2018).

_____, 2018b, *Cosmos Creation: The Unified SuperStandard Model, Volume 2, SECOND EDITION* (Pingree Hill Publishing, Auburn, NH, 2018).

_____, 2018c, *God Theory (*Pingree Hill Publishing, Auburn, NH, 2018).

_____, 2018d, *Immortal Eye: God Theory: Second Edition* (Pingree Hill Publishing, Auburn, NH, 2018).

_____, 2018e, *Unification of God Theory and Unified SuperStandard Model THIRD EDITION* (Pingree Hill Publishing, Auburn, NH, 2018).

_____, 2019a, *Calculation of: QED α = 1/137, and Other Coupling Constants of the Unified SuperStandard Theory* (Pingree Hill Publishing, Auburn, NH, 2019).

_____, 2019b, *Coupling Constants of the Unified SuperStandard Theory SECOND EDITION* (Pingree Hill Publishing, Auburn, NH, 2019).

_____, 2019c, *New Hybrid Quantum Big_Bang–Megaverse_Driven Universe with a Finite Big Bang and an Increasing Hubble Constant* (Pingree Hill Publishing, Auburn, NH, 2019).

_____, 2019d, *The Universe, The Electron and The Vacuum* (Pingree Hill Publishing, Auburn, NH, 2019).

_____, 2019e, *Quantum Big Bang – Quantum Vacuum Universes (Particles)* (Pingree Hill Publishing, Auburn, NH, 2019).

_____, 2019f, *The Exact QED Calculation of the Fine Structure Constant Implies ALL 4D Universes have the Same Physics/Life Prospects* (Pingree Hill Publishing, Auburn, NH, 2019).

_____, 2019g, *Unified SuperStandard Theory and the SuperUniverse Model: The Foundation of Science* (Pingree Hill Publishing, Auburn, NH, 2019).

_____, 2020a, *Quaternion Unified SuperStandard Theory (The QUeST) and Megaverse Octonion SuperStandard Theory (MOST)* (Pingree Hill Publishing, Auburn, NH, 2020).

_____, 2020b, *United Universes Quaternion Universe - Octonion Megaverse* (Pingree Hill Publishing, Auburn, NH, 2020).

_____, 2020c, *Unified SuperStandard Theories for Quaternion Universes & The Octonion Megaverse* (Pingree Hill Publishing, Auburn, NH, 2020).

_____, 2020d, *The Essence of Eternity: Quaternion & Octonion SuperStandard Theories* (Pingree Hill Publishing, Auburn, NH, 2020).

Bucke, R. M., 1901, *Cosmic Consciousness* (Innes & Sons, New York, 1901).

Eddington, A. S., 1952, *The Mathematical Theory of Relativity* (Cambridge University Press, Cambridge, U.K., 1952).

Fant, Karl M., 2005, *Logically Determined Design: Clockless System Design With NULL Convention Logic* (John Wiley and Sons, Hoboken, NJ, 2005).

Feinberg, G. and Shapiro, R., 1980, *Life Beyond Earth: The Intelligent Earthlings Guide to Life in the Universe* (William Morrow and Company, New York, 1980).

Gelfand, I. M., Fomin, S. V., Silverman, R. A. (tr), 2000, *Calculus of Variations* (Dover Publications, Mineola, NY, 2000).

Giaquinta, M., Modica, G., Souchek, J., 1998, *Cartesian Coordinates in the Calculus of Variations* Volumes I and II (Springer-Verlag, New York, 1998).

Giaquinta, M., Hildebrandt, S., 1996, *Calculus of Variations* Volumes I and II (Springer-Verlag, New York, 1996).

Gradshteyn, I. S. and Ryzhik, I. M., 1965, *Table of Integrals, Series, and Products* (Academic Press, New York, 1965).

Heitler, W., 1954, *The Quantum Theory of Radiation* (Claendon Press, Oxford, UK, 1954).

Huang, Kerson, 1992, *Quarks, Leptons & Gauge Fields 2nd Edition* (World Scientific Publishing Company, Singapore, 1992).

Jost, J., Li-Jost, X., 1998, *Calculus of Variations* (Cambridge University Press, New York, 1998).

Kaku, Michio, 1993, *Quantum Field Theory*, (Oxford University Press, New York, 1993).

Kirk, G. S. and Raven, J. E., 1962, *The Presocratic Philosophers* (Cambridge University Press, New York, 1962).

Landau, L. D. and Lifshitz, E. M., 1987, *Fluid Mechanics 2nd Edition*, (Pergamon Press, Elmsford, NY, 1987).

Misner, C. W., Thorne, K. S., and Wheeler, J. A., 1973, *Gravitation* (W. H. Freeman, New York, 1973).

Rescher, N., 1967, *The Philosophy of Leibniz* (Prentice-Hall, Englewood Cliffs, NJ, 1967).

Rieffel, Eleanor and Polak, Wolfgang, 2014, *Quantum Computing* (MIT Press, Cambridge, MA, 2014).

Riesz, Frigyes and Sz.-Nagy, Béla, 1990, *Functional Analysis* (Dover Publications, New York, 1990).

Sagan, H., 1993, *Introduction to the Calculus of Variations* (Dover Publications, Mineola, NY, 1993).

Sakurai, J. J., 1964, *Invariance Principles and Elementary Particles* (Princeton University Press, Princeton, NJ, 1964).

Sorokin, Pitirim, 1941, *Social and Cultural Dynamics* (Porter Sargent Publishers, Boston, MA, 1941).

Streater, R. F. and Wightman, A. S., 2000, *PCT, Spin, Statistics, and All That* (Princeton University Press, Princeton, NJ 2000).

Weinberg, S., 1972, *Gravitation and Cosmology* (John Wiley and Sons, New York, 1972).

Weinberg, S., 1995, *The Quantum Theory of Fields Volume I* (Cambridge University Press, New York, 1995).

Weinberg, S., 2000, *The Quantum Theory of Fields Volume III Supersymmetry* (Cambridge University Press, New York, 2000).

Weyl, H., 1950, *Space, Time, Matter* (Dover, New York, 1950).

Weyl, H., (Tr. S. Pollard et al), 1987, *The Continuum* (Dover Publications, New York, 1987).

INDEX

absolute reality, 48
Black Hole, 60
brain size, 54
Bucke, 51
Chomsky, 41, 42
Complex General Relativity, 61, 62
complex quaternion space, 3, 4, 5, 6, 7, 8, 9, 13, 17, 19, 24, 25, 26, 27
computer memory, 55
connectivity, 55
Consciousness Platform, 54
Cosmic Consciousness, 51
Cosmos, iv, 64, 73
Creation, 64
Dark Energy, 60
Dark Matter, 60, 61, 62
Dark U(4) group, 15
dimension rules, 6
divergences, 72
dynamically refigure, 55
Einstein, Podolsky, and Rosen, 27
ElectroWeak, 60
EPR, 27, 29, 30
Feynman Path Integrals, 39, 40
fine structure constant, 73
four layer MOST, 16
four layer QUeST, 7
Functional Byte Numbering, 33
Generation group, 11
Higgs Mechanism, 62, 72
Higgs particles, 72
instantaneous action-at-a-distance, 27
interactions, 72
Intrinsic Consciousness, 52
Inventive Consciousness, 52
Justification for a Four Layer MOST, 17
Justification for a Four Layer QUeST, 7
Landauer mass, 35, 36
Layer group, 11
Leibniz, 66, 67
LHC, iv, 61
Mathematical Picture Language, 3
Megaverse, iv, 64, 65
MOST, iv, 10, 16, 17, 18, 65
nonterminal, 41, 42
observability, 47
Parity Violation, 60
pebbles, 3
Perturbation Theory Divergences, 24
Production Rules, 42, 43, 44
psiphi, 3, 4, 6, 13
Pythagoras, 3
Quantum, 64, 72, 74

quantum computers, 72
Quantum Entanglement, 34, 62
quantum functional, 30
quark, 72
quba, 34, 35, 37, 38
qubas, 37, 39, 47
qube, 29, 34, 35, 36
qubes, 34, 35, 37, 39, 47
QUeST, iv, 3, 5, 6, 7, 8, 9, 10, 16, 17, 19, 21, 24, 25, 32, 65, 74
Self Consciousness, 51
Simple Consciousness, 51
Special Relativity, 60
spin, 72
SU(3), 60

SuperStandard Model, iv, 64, 65
SuperSymmetry, 64
symbols, 41, 42
terminal, 41, 42
Theory of Everything, 59, 62
U(4), 61, 62
U(8), 62
Unified SuperStandard Model, iv, 64, 65
UST, 1, 3, 5, 6, 7, 8, 10, 18, 19, 21, 22, 23, 24, 25, 74
Wave Space, 37
Web of Galaxies, 61

About the Author

Stephen Blaha is a well-known Physicist and Man of Letters with interests in Science, Society and civilization, the Arts, and Technology. He had an Alfred P. Sloan Foundation scholarship in college. He received his Ph.D. in Physics from Rockefeller University. He has served on the faculties of several major universities. He was also a Member of the Technical Staff at Bell Laboratories, a manager at the Boston Globe Newspaper, a Director at Wang Laboratories, and President of Blaha Software Inc. and of Janus Associates Inc. (NH).

Among other achievements he was a co-discoverer of the "r potential" for heavy quark binding developing the first (and still the only demonstrable) non-Aeolian gauge theory with an "r" potential; first suggested the existence of topological structures in superfluid He-3; first proposed Yang-Mills theories would appear in condensed matter phenomena with non-scalar order parameters; first developed a grammar-based formalism for quantum computers and applied it to elementary particle theories; first developed a new form of quantum field theory without divergences (thus solving a major 60 year old problem that enabled a unified theory of the Standard Model and Quantum Gravity without divergences to be developed); first developed a formulation of complex General Relativity based on analytic continuation from real space-time; first developed a generalized non-homogeneous Robertson-Walker metric that enabled a quantum theory of the Big Bang to be developed without singularities at $t = 0$; first generalized Cauchy's theorem and Gauss' theorem to complex, curved multi-dimensional spaces; received Honorable Mention in the Gravity Research Foundation Essay Competition in 1978; first developed a physically acceptable theory of faster-than-light particles; first derived a composition of extremums method in the Calculus of Variations; first quantitatively suggested that inflationary periods in the history of the universe were not needed; first proved Gödel's Theorem implies Nature must be quantum; provided a new alternative to the Higgs Mechanism, and Higgs particles, to generate masses; first showed how to resolve logical paradoxes including Gödel's Undecidability Theorem by developing Operator Logic and Quantum Operator Logic; first developed a quantitative harmonic oscillator-like model of the life cycle, and interactions, of civilizations; first showed how equations describing superorganisms also apply to civilizations. A recent book shows his theory applies successfully to the past 14 years of history and to *new* archaeological data on Andean and Mayan civilizations as well as Early Anatolian and Egyptian civilizations.

He first developed an axiomatic derivation of the form of The Standard Model from geometry – space-time properties – The Unified SuperStandard Model. It unifies all the known forces of Nature. It also has a Dark Matter sector that includes a Dark ElectroWeak sector with Dark doublets and Dark gauge interactions. It uses quantum coordinates to remove infinities that crop up in most interacting quantum field theories and additionally to remove the infinities that appear in the Big Bang and generate inflationary growth of the universe. It shows

gravity has a MOND-like form without sacrificing Newton's Laws. It relates the interactions of the MOND-like sector of gravity with the r-potential of Quark Confinement. The axioms of the theory lead to the question of their origin. We suggest in the preceding edition of this book it can be attributed to an entity with God-like properties. We explore these properties in "God Theory" and show they predict that the Cosmos exists forever although individual universes (or incarnations of our universe) "come and go." Several other important results emerge from God Theory such a functionally triune God. The Unified SuperStandard Theory has many other important parts described in the Current Edition of *The Unified SuperStandard Theory* and expanded in subsequent volumes.

Blaha has had a major impact on a succession of elementary particle theories: his Ph.D. thesis (1970), and papers, showed that quantum field theory calculations to all orders in ladder approximations could not give scaling deep inelastic electron-nucleon scattering. He later showed the eigenvalue equation for the fine structure constant α in Johnson-Baker-Willey QED had a zero at $\alpha = 1$ not 1/137 by solving the Schwinger-Dyson equations to all orders in an approximation that agreed with exact results to 4th order in α thus ending interest in this theory. In 1979 at Prof. Ken Johnson's (MIT) suggestion he calculated the proton-neutron mass difference in the MIT bag model and found the result had the wrong sign reducing interest in the bag model. These results all appear in Physical Review papers. In the 2000's he repeatedly pointed out the shortcomings of SuperString theory and showed that The Standard Model's form could be derived from space-time geometry by an extension of Lorentz transformations to faster than light transformations. This deeper space-time basis greatly increases the possibility that it is part of THE fundamental theory. Recently, Blaha showed that the Weak interactions differed significantly from the Strong, electromagnetic and gravitation interactions in important respects while these interactions had similar features, and suggested that ElectroWeak theory, which is essentially a glued union of the Weak interactions and Electromagnetism, possibly modulo unknown Higgs particle features, be replaced by a unified theory of the other interactions combined with a stand-alone Weak interaction theory. Blaha also showed that, if Charmonium calculations are taken seriously, the Strong interaction coupling constant is only a factor of five larger than the electromagnetic coupling constant, and thus Strong interaction perturbation theory would make sense and yield physically meaningful results.

In graduate school (1965-71) he wrote substantial papers in elementary particles and group theory: The Inelastic E- P Structure Functions in a Gluon Model. Phys. Lett. B40:501-502,1972; Deep-Inelastic E-P Structure Functions In A Ladder Model With Spin 1/2 Nucleons, Phys.Rev. D3:510-523,1971; Continuum Contributions To The Pion Radius, Phys. Rev. 178:2167-2169,1969; Character Analysis of U(N) and SU(N), J. Math. Phys. <u>10</u>, 2156 (1969); and The Calculation of the Irreducible Characters of the Symmetric Group in Terms of the Compound Characters, (Published as Blaha's Lemma in D. E. Knuth's book: *The Art of Computer Programming Vols. 1 – 4*).

In the early 1980's Blaha was also a pioneer in the development of UNIX for financial, scientific and Internet applications: benchmarked UNIX versions showing that block size was critical for UNIX performance, developing financial modeling software, starting database benchmarking comparison studies, developing Internet-like UNIX networking (1982) and developing a hybrid shell programming technique (1982) that was a precursor to the PERL programming language. He was also the manager of the AT&T ten-year future products development database. His work helped lead to commercial UNIX on computers such as Sun Micros, IBM AIX minis, and Apple computers.

In the 1980's he pioneered the development of PC Desktop Publishing on laser printers. and was nominated for three "Awards for Technical Excellence" in 1987 by PC Magazine for PC software products that he designed and developed.

Recently he has developed a theory of Megaverses – actual universes of which our universe is one – with quantum particle-like properties based on the Wheeler-DeWitt equation of Quantum Gravity. He has developed a theory of a baryonic force, which had been conjectured many years ago, and estimated the strength of the force based on discrepancies in measurements of the gravitational constant G. This force, operative in D-dimensional space, can be used to escape from our universe in "uniships" which are the equivalent of the faster-than-light starships proposed in the author's earlier books. Thus travel to other universes, as well as to other stars is possible.

Blaha also considered the complexified Wheeler-DeWitt equation and showed that its limitation to real-valued coordinates and metrics generated a Cosmological Constant in the Einstein equations.

The author has also recently written a series of books on the serious problems of the United States and their solution as well as a book on the decline of Mankind that will follow from current social and genetic trends in Mankind.

In the past twenty years Dr. Blaha has written over 80 books on a wide range of topics. Some recent major works are: *From Asynchronous Logic to The Standard Model to Superflight to the Stars, All the Universe!, SuperCivilizations: Civilizations as Superorganisms, America's Future: an Islamic Surge, ISIS, al Qaeda, World Epidemics, Ukraine, Russia-China Pact, US Leadership Crisis, The Rises and Falls of Man – Destiny – 3000 AD: New Support for a Superorganism MACRO-THEORY of CIVILIZATIONS From CURRENT WORLD TRENDS and NEW Peruvian, Pre-Mayan, Mayan, Anatolian, and Early Egyptian Data, with a Projection to 3000 AD,* and *Mankind in Decline: Genetic Disasters, Human-Animal Hybrids, Overpopulation, Pollution, Global Warming, Food and Water Shortages, Desertification, Poverty, Rising Violence, Genocide, Epidemics, Wars, Leadership Failure.*

He has taught approximately 4,000 students in undergraduate, graduate, and postgraduate corporate education courses primarily in major universities, and large companies and government agencies.

Recently he developed a quantum theory, The Unified SuperStandard Theory (UST), which describes elementary particles in detail without the difficulties of conventional quantum field theory. He found that the internal symmetries of this theory could be exactly derived from a 32 dimension complex quaternion theory called QUeST. He further found that a 32 dimension complex octonion theory (MOST) describes the Megaverse. It can hold QUeST universes such as our own universe. It has an internal symmetry structure which is a superset of the QUeST internal symmetries.

www.ingramcontent.com/pod-product-compliance
Lightning Source LLC
Chambersburg PA
CBHW081348040426
42450CB00015B/3351